CATHOLIC SCHOOLS AND THE LAW OF SPECIAL EDUCATION:
A Reference Guide

Charles J. Russo, M.Div., JD, EdD
Rev. Joseph D. Massucci, PhD
Allan G. Osborne, Jr., EdD
Gerald M. Cattaro, EdD

National Catholic Educational Association

Copyright 2002
National Catholic Educational Association
1077 30th Street, NW, Suite 100
Washington, DC 20007-3852
ISBN 1-55833-273-1

Table of Contents

Dedication

This book is dedicated to our parents:

James J. and Helen J. Russo
Vincent James and Martha Ann Massucci
Allan G. and Ruth L. Osborne
Vito and Lucy Cattaro

Acknowledgments

The authors would like to acknowledge and thank all those who helped with this book. Great appreciation is expressed to the reviewers who provided very useful comments and suggestions: Dr. Ralph D. Mawdsley, Professor at Cleveland State University in Cleveland, OH; Dr. Nelda Cambron McCabe, Professor at Miami University of Ohio in Oxford, OH; Ms. Jane Goff, Assistant Principal at St. Mary's High School in St. Louis, MO; Dr. Antoinette Dudek, Associate Executive Director of Early Childhood and Special Education Services in the NCEA Department of Elementary Schools in Washington, DC; Sr. Dale McDonald, PBVM, PhD, Director of Public Policy and Educational Research at NCEA in Washington, DC. Special thanks also goes to Ms. Elizabeth Pearn at the University of Dayton for her work on the book. Thank you also to Sr. Mary Frances Taymans, SND, EdD, Executive Director of the NCEA Secondary Schools Department and to Brian Vaccaro for their guidance on and work with this publication.

Foreword

Educating students with special needs is very important. It is also a very complex endeavor due to the many legal requirements and restrictions that exist. *Catholic Schools and the Law of Special Education: A Reference Guide* is an excellent resource on the legal aspects of special education. The authors, Dr. Charles J. Russo, Rev. Joseph D. Massucci, Dr. Allan G. Osborne, and Dr. Gerald M. Cattaro, thoroughly examine special education, Section 504 of the Rehabilitation Act of 1973, and the Individuals with Disabilities Education Act (IDEA). Their clear and concise explanations make complicated and difficult issues easier to understand.

The book divides into two major parts. Chapters one through four look at special education, Section 504 of the Rehabilitation Act of 1973, and the Individuals with Disabilities Education Act from the legal perspective. Here, the authors explain special education, provide a brief history of it, and examine several key court cases. Section 504 and IDEA are examined in depth. Under Section 504, the authors explain what the law addresses and what must be done in compliance with it, including admissions examinations and standards as well as service plans. An explanation of IDEA is also provided. The authors address ten key issues including private and residential school placement, extended school year programs, related services, assistive technology, and discipline. Under each of the issues, what must be done by law for students with special needs is spelled out.

Chapters five through eight examine special education as it affects religiously affiliated non-public schools. In light of the 1997 IDEA Amendments and the 1999 regulations, the authors address how these institutions and their students with special needs fit within the laws' requirements. They then address several key issues specifically facing Catholic school administrators including working with parents and public school officials, providing staff development, and assessing the classroom setting.

The appendices contain several valuable resources: the text of *Welcome and Justice for Persons with Disabilities*, the United States Bishops' statement on individuals with disabilities, selected relevant federal regulations, and a list of useful special education web sites.

Questions and difficulties often arise when dealing with students with special needs. It is important that Catholic school administrators, teachers, and parents understand the law, its requirements, and the services that must be provided for these students. *Catholic Schools and the Law of Special Education: A Reference Guide* is an excellent resource for all those who are called to work with students with special needs.

Brian Vaccaro
Editor
NCEA Secondary Schools Department

I. Introduction

Beginning with their landmark statement, *To Teach As Jesus Did: A Pastoral Message on Catholic Education*, the American Catholic bishops acknowledged that "[t]he right of the handicapped to receive religious education adapted to their special needs also challenges the ingenuity and commitment of the Catholic community."[1] Although primarily addressing religious education outside of the regular programs in Catholic elementary and secondary schools, the bishops presciently recognized and sought to take steps to meet the needs of the disabled.[2] The present challenge facing Roman Catholic elementary and secondary schools is how to meet the needs of growing numbers of parents who wish to provide their children with disabilities with the benefits of a Catholic school education.[3]

Even in the absence of clear data on the number of parents wishing to have their children with disabilities attend Catholic schools, there are significant numbers of students with such needs. For example, an NCEA report reveals that of the 397 Catholic schools that responded to a national survey, each reported the presence of about fourteen students with disabilities. More specifically, this report indicates that schools had the following percentages per disability: 79.4% with learning disabilities; 74.2% with attention deficit disorder/attention deficit/hyperactivity disorder; 73.7% with speech impairments; 24.9% with hearing impairments; 20.0% with emotional/behavioral disabilities; 19.6% with physical disabilities; 15.3%

with visual impairments; and 10.8% with autism/non-language learning disorders.[4]

In their most recent pronouncement on the needs of children and adults with disabilities, in November 1998, the bishops weighed in with their eloquent statement, *Welcome and Justice for Persons with Disabilities.* In the sections most relevant to Catholic elementary and secondary schools, the bishops declared that:

> *Defense of the right to life implies the defense of all other rights which enable the individual with the disability to achieve the fullest measure of personal development of which he or she is capable. These include the right to equal opportunity in education. . . .*

> *Since the parish is the door to participation in the Christian experience, it is the responsibility of both pastors and laity to assure that those doors are always open. Costs must never be the controlling consideration limiting the welcome offered to those among us with disabilities, since provision of access to religious functions is a pastoral duty.*[5]

As educational leaders in Catholic schools take the needs of children with disabilities into consideration, they can easily find themselves on the horns of a dilemma. On the one hand is the desire of Catholic educators to satisfy parents by meeting the educational needs of their children. On the other hand is the realistic challenge of seeking to comply with the bishops' concern that cost not become an issue when the financial ramifications of including children with disabilities can be significant. Educational leaders in Catholic schools have reason for concern, not without cause, that offering a special education program may have a significant impact not only on a school and the majority of its students but also on its budget and parish resources.[6] The situation is complicated by virtue of the fact that Catholic schools are not legally obligated to accept children with disabilities.[7]

Even though Catholic schools are not legally bound to accept students with disabilities, it would be consistent with Church teaching to do so and would give powerful witness to the faith by making schools more accessible to these children. Consequently, it is important for educators, and all others who are interested in Catholic schools, to be well acquainted with broad-based statutory rights of children with disabilities, most notably Section 504 of the Rehabilitation Act of 1973 (Section 504)[8] and the Individuals with Disabilities Education Act (IDEA),[9] especially since these laws, like virtually all legal matters, continue to evolve.[10]

It is particularly important for educators in Catholic schools to have an awareness and understanding of Section 504 and the IDEA because even if these laws do not always directly apply in Catholic schools, parents who wish to place their children in Catholic schools are increasingly knowledgeable about the statutory entitlements that their children might have received had they attended public schools. Many parents also have growing understandings of the extent to which some of the services under Section 504 and the IDEA might be available to their children who attend Catholic schools.

Of the two statutes, Section 504 is the more far-reaching since it covers students, staff, and even visitors in schools and at school activities (as well as at other places). The IDEA, on the other hand, is designed to provide a free appropriate public education to all students with disabilities in the least restrictive environment. Subject to its defense provisions, Section 504 applies to students in public and Catholic schools even though it does not provide direct financial assistance to school officials as they must develop policies and practices that comply with its dictates. Conversely, while children with disabilities who are covered by the IDEA are occasionally enrolled in, and receive services at, Catholic schools, this comprehensive statute has no direct application to students whose parents voluntarily enroll them in Catholic and other religiously affiliated non-public schools since this law involves direct federal financial assistance. Yet, federal law does not prevent states from providing additional special education programs and services in Catholic schools under their own laws.[11] To the extent that the IDEA places the obligation on the state, *qua* public schools, to ensure that each child with a disability receives a free appropriate public education,[12] all of those interested in Catholic education, including diocesan officials, pastors, school administrators, staff, parents, and interested parishoners will be well served to have a basic understanding of this complex statute and its regulations.

In light of legal issues surrounding the delivery of special education to children who attend Catholic schools,[13] this book is divided into eight sections.[14] Following this introduction is a brief history of special education. The next sections review Section 504 and the IDEA, particularly focusing on recent changes in the law and implementing regulations, before examining issues in need of further clarification concerning the delivery of special education to children who attend Catholic schools. The penultimate section of the text offers practical considerations for educators in Catholic elementary and secondary schools as they think about implementing special education programs. The book ends with a brief conclusion. The authors fervently hope that the text will provide interested readers with a better understanding of the relevant statutes, regulations, and cases that will assist them in their quest to better provide for the delivery of special education to children who attend Catholic schools.

II. History of Special Education

Perhaps the most important case involving American Catholic schools was *Pierce v. Society of Sisters (Pierce)*,[15] wherein the Supreme Court ruled that parents could satisfy a state's compulsory attendance law by sending their children to a religiously affiliated non-public school. *Pierce*, which can be considered a Magna Carta of sorts for religious freedom, helped to ensure religious freedom in education by recognizing the right of Catholic and other non-public schools to operate. In the years since *Pierce*, Catholic schools have undeniably contributed greatly to ensuring equal educational opportunities for millions of students throughout the United States.[16]

On a broader basis, the impetus for ensuring equal educational opportunities for all American children can be traced to *Brown v. Board of Education, Topeka (Brown)*.[17] Although resolved in the context of school desegregation, in *Brown* the Supreme Court set the tone for later developments including those leading to protecting the rights of students with disabilities in its assertion that "[e]ducation is perhaps the most important function of state and local governments."[18]

In the years following *Brown*, an attitude of not always so benign neglect remained in effect with regard to the disabled. In fact, throughout the 1950s, twenty-eight states had laws requiring the sterilization of individuals with disabilities while others limited such basic rights as voting, marrying, and obtaining a driver's license.[19] By the 1960s, the percentages of children with disabilities who were served in public schools began to rise; the 12% of children in public schools in 1948 increased to 21% in 1963 and to 38% in 1968.[20] As of July 1, 1974, the Bureau for the Education of the Handicapped reported that about 78.5% of the nation's 8,150,000 eligible children with disabilities received some form of public education. Of these children, 47.8% received special education and related services, 30.7% did not receive related services, and the remaining 21.5% did not receive educational services at all.[21]

Statistical data aside, a major push for the development of special education came in two federal cases that set the stage for subsequent statutory developments. In *Pennsylvania Association for Retarded Children v. Pennsylvania (PARC),*[22] a federal trial court, in a consent decree, established the bases for what developed into the IDEA. In *PARC,* the parties agreed not only that children with disabilities could neither be denied admission to a public school nor be subjected to a change in educational placement unless their parents received procedural due process but also that a placement in a regular school classroom was preferable to one in a more restrictive setting. *PARC* in addition recognized that children with disabilities could learn in a school setting. Similarly, in *Mills v. Board of Education of the District of Columbia (Mills),*[23] a federal trial court ruled that despite the school system's claims that it lacked the resources for all of its students, it could not deny services to children with disabilities and that they could not be excluded from public schools without receiving due process. Insofar as *Mills* originated in Washington, DC, it was probably among the more significant influences moving federal law makers to act to ensure adequate protection for children with disabilities when they adopted Section 504 and the IDEA.

In light of legal developments following *PARC* and *Mills,* the following sections of the book review major statutory developments under Section 504 and the IDEA aimed at safeguarding the educational rights of children with disabilities. In the wake of the literally thousands of suits that have been filed in federal and state courts, only a small portion of which involve Catholic schools, selected cases are discussed under the appropriate headings rather than as separate entries.

III. Section 504 of the Rehabilitation Act of 1973

The Rehabilitation Act of 1973, part of a much older statute that traces its origins to World War I, was the first federal civil rights law protecting the rights of the disabled. Among its provisions, Section 504 declares that "[n]o otherwise qualified individual with a disability in the United States . . . shall, solely by reason of her or his disability, be excluded from the participation in, be denied the benefits of, or be subjected to discrimination under any program or activity receiving [f]ederal financial assistance . . . ."[24]

Section 504, which is not predicated on an institution's receipt of federal financial assistance,[25] is applicable to Catholic schools[26] because this term is construed so broadly and offers broad-based protection to individuals under the more amorphous concept of impairment rather than disability.[27] It is important to note that while Section 504 covers students, employees, and others, this book focuses on the rights of children. Section 504 defines an individual with a disability as one "who (i) has a physical or mental impairment which substantially limits one or more of such a person's major life activities, (ii) has a record of such an impairment, or (iii) is regarded as having such an impairment."[28]

In order to have a record of impairment, an individual must have a history of, or been identified as having, a mental or physical impairment that substantially limits one or more major life activities,[29] including schooling.[30] Once a student is identified as having a disability, the next step is to determine whether he or she is "otherwise qualified." In order to be "otherwise qualified," as the term is applied to preschool, elementary, and secondary school students, a child must be "(i) of an age during which nonhandicapped persons are provided such services, (ii) of any age during which it is mandatory under state law to provide such services to handicapped persons, or (iii) [a student] to whom a state is required to provide a free appropriate public education [under the IDEA]."[31] An individual who is "otherwise qualified," meaning that he or she is eligible to participate in a program or activity despite the existence of an impairment, must be permitted to participate in the program or activity as long as it is possible to do so by means of a "reasonable accommodation."[32]

> *A reasonable accommodation may involve minor adjustments such as permitting a child to be accompanied by a service dog, modifying a behavior policy to accommodate a student with an autoimmune disease who is disruptive, or providing a hearing interpreter for a student.*

A reasonable accommodation may involve minor[33] adjustments such as permitting a child to be accompanied by a service dog,[34] modifying a behavior policy to accommodate a student with an autoimmune disease who is disruptive,[35] or providing a hearing interpreter for a student.[36] Academic modifications might include permitting a child a longer period of time to complete an examination or assignment, using peer tutors, distributing outlines in advance, employing specialized curricular materials, and/or permitting students to use laptop computers to record answers on examinations. In modifying facilities, school officials do not have to make every classroom and/or area of a building accessible; it may be enough to bring services to a child such as offering a keyboard for musical instruction rather than revamping an entire music room for a student who wishes to take piano classes.[37]

Even if a child appears to be "otherwise qualified," school officials can rely on one of three defenses to avoid being charged with noncompliance of Section 504. This represents a major difference between Section 504 and the IDEA since no such defenses are applicable under the latter.[38] Moreover, it is important to recognize that the courts generally defer to educational decision making in this arena.[39] First, schools can be excused from making accommodations that would result in "a fundamental alteration in the nature of [a] program."[40] For example, permitting a high school student to take fewer classes, over a six-year period, rather than over the usual four years, would most likely be such a major modification. The second defense permits school officials to avoid compliance if a modification imposes "undue financial burden[s]."[41] In other words, if the cost of providing a service needed by a child, such as an aide to assist with class work, would have a significant financial impact on a school's budget, then it probably would not be required under Section 504. The third defense is that an otherwise qualified student with a disability can be excluded from a program if his or her presence creates a substantial risk of injury to himself, herself, or others.[42] For example, a child with a spastic condition could possibly be excluded from a class that meets in a chemistry laboratory due to fears of being injured while working near the flames of a bunsen burner. However, in order to comply with Section 504, school officials would probably have to offer a reasonable accommodation such as providing a computer assisted program to accomplish an instructional goal similar to the one that would have been achieved in a laboratory class.

> *Section 504 also prohibits discrimination by requiring educators to make individualized modifications for otherwise qualified students with disabilities. This means that all schools, including Catholic schools, assuming that they have admitted children pursuant to Section 504, must provide aid, benefits, and/or services that are comparable to those available to students who are not disabled.*

Section 504 also prohibits discrimination by requiring educators to make individualized modifications for otherwise qualified students with disabilities. This means that all schools, including Catholic schools, assuming that they have admitted children pursuant to Section 504, must provide aid, benefits, and/or services that are comparable to those available to students who are not disabled. As such, children with disabilities must receive comparable materials, teacher quality, length of school term, and daily hours of instruction. These programs should not be separate from those available to students who are not disabled unless such segregation is necessary for a program to be effective. Further, while schools are not prohibited from offering separate programs for students with disabilities, these children cannot be required to attend such classes unless they cannot be served adequately in such a setting.[43] If such programs are offered separately, facilities must, of course, be comparable.[44] If a school offers a special program for students with disabilities, it may not charge more for such services "except to the extent that any additional charge is justified by a substantial increase in cost."[45]

Once identified, each qualified student with a disability is entitled to an appropriate public education, regardless of the nature or severity of his or her disability. In order to guarantee that an appropriate education is made available, Section 504's regulations include due process requirements for evaluation and placement similar to, but not nearly as extensive as, those under the IDEA.[46]

Finally, Section 504, which is enforced by the Office of Civil Rights, requires each recipient of federal financial aid to file an assurance of compliance; provide notice to students and their parents that their programs are nondiscriminatory; engage in remedial actions where violations are proven; take voluntary steps to overcome the effects of conditions that resulted in limiting the participation of students with disabilities in their programs; conduct a self- evaluation; designate a staff member, typically at the central office level, as compliance coordinator; and adopt grievance procedures.[47]

Admissions Examinations/Standards

In a related vein, it is worth keeping in mind that Catholic schools in some parts of the United States, including those that consider admitting students with disabilities, require applicants to take an admission examination and/or be interviewed prior to acceptance or placement[48] in order to determine whether they are otherwise qualified.[49] Under Section 504, schools relying on examinations or interviews may be required to provide reasonable accommodations to applicants who are disabled. While school officials are not required to alter the content of an examination or an interview, they may have to make accommodations in how a test is administered or an interview is conducted. In other words, school officials would not be required to make an examination easier so that students who simply lacked the requisite knowledge could pass,[50] but they may have to alter the conditions under which an examination is administered, or an interview is conducted, so that a student with a disability with the requisite knowledge and skills to pass or express himself or herself fully can do so in spite of his or her disability.

Accommodations for an examination may be as simple as providing a quiet room without distractions, essentially a private room away from others, for a student who suffers from attention deficit hyperactivity disorder or procuring the services of a reader or a braille version of an examination for an applicant who is blind. Additionally, a student with a physical disability may require special seating arrangements, a scribe to record answers to questions, and/or being permitted to use a laptop (or desktop) computer to record answers on examinations. Similarly, whether as part of an examination or admissions interview, a student who is hearing impaired might be entitled to the services of a sign-language interpreter to communicate directions that are normally given orally. At the same time, school officials may be required to provide a student with a learning disability with extra time in which to complete an examination or make a computer available to a child who may be more comfortable with one than with a traditional paper and pencil test.

Prior to receiving an accommodation, a student must prove that he or she is, for example, learning disabled[51] and that the extra time to take an examination is necessary due to the learning disability.[52] Again, the purpose of providing the extra time would be to allow the student, who might have difficulty processing information, sufficient opportunity to show that he or she is capable of answering the questions. It is the responsibility of a student (and his or her parent(s)) to make school officials aware of the fact that he or she is disabled and needs testing or interviewing accommodations. To this end, principals and other school officials should require proof that a student has a disability in need of accommodation in order for him or her to demonstrate knowledge and skills on the examination. A student, through his or her parent(s), should also suggest which accommodations would be most appropriate. In considering whether a student is entitled to accommodations, school officials must make individualized inquiries. School officials would violate Section 504 if they refused to make testing accommodations or made modifications only for students with certain specified disabilities.

Section 504 Service Plans

As noted, students who qualify under the Section 504 definition are entitled to reasonable accommodations so that they may access a school's programs. Making accommodations may involve alterations to the physical plant, such as building wheelchair ramps or removing architectural barriers, so that students may physically enter and get around the school building.[53] School officials must also allow students to bring service dogs into the classroom[54] but are not required to provide accommodations that go beyond what would be considered reasonable. As noted under the defense to Section 504, accommodations that are excessively expensive, expose the school's staff to excessive risk, or that require a school to make a substantial modification to the mission or purpose of a program would not be required.[55]

Although not specifically required by Section 504, many schools spell out the accommodations and services that will be provided to an eligible student in a written service plan. Even though a written service plan is not mandated by federal law, the components of a service plan are likewise not required. Even so, in practical terms, the following components should be included in a written Section 504 service plan:

> **Demographic Data** - Student's name, date of birth, school identification number, grade, school, teacher, parents' names, address, telephone number, and the like;

> **Team Members** - A listing of all team members, and their

respective roles, who contributed to the development of the service plan;

Disability - A description of the student's disability and its severity along with an explanation of how it impedes the child's educational progress; and

Accommodations and Services - A detailed description of the accommodations and services to be offered under the plan, including the frequency and location of services and when they will be provided.

In addition, any evaluative reports or assessments that helped to determine the nature of a student's disability and the need for accommodations and services should be attached.

IV. Individuals with Disabilities Education Act

U nlike Section 504, which has fairly broad standards, in order to qualify for services under the IDEA, originally named the Education for All Handicapped Children Act when it was first enacted in 1975,[56] a child with a disability must meet three statutory requirements. First, a child must be between the ages of three and twenty-one.[57] Second, a child must have a specifically identified disability.[58] Third, a child must be in need of special education,[59] meaning that he or she must be in need of a free appropriate education (FAPE)[60] in the least restrictive environment that conforms to an individualized education program (IEP).[61]

An IEP must contain statements of a student's current educational performance, annual goals and short term objectives, the specific educational services to be provided, the extent to which the child can participate in general education, the date of initiation and duration of services, and criteria to evaluate whether the objectives are being met.[62] An IEP must also include statements concerning how a child's disability affects his or her ability to be involved in and progress in the general educational curriculum along with statements regarding any modifications that may be needed to allow the child to participate in the general curriculum. If necessary, each child with a disability is entitled to related services[63] to assist him or her in benefiting from an IEP.[64]

The IDEA includes an elaborate system of procedural safeguards to protect the rights of children and their parents.[65] In addition, the IDEA includes provisions, supplemented by the Family Education Rights and Privacy Act[66] and its accompanying regulations,[67] preserving the confidentiality of all information used in the evaluation, placement, and education of students. Pursuant to these safeguards, the parent(s) of a child with a disability must be afforded the opportunity to participate in the development of the IEP for and placement of their child.[68] Further, the IDEA requires school officials to provide written notice and obtain parental consent prior to evaluating a child[69] or making an initial placement.[70] After a student has been placed in special education, school board officials must provide the parent(s) with proper notice before initiating a change in placement.[71] Once placed, a child's situation must be reviewed at least annually[72] and the student must be re-evaluated completely at least every three years.[73]

Under the IDEA, the parent(s) of a student with a disability may be entitled to an independent evaluation at public expense if they disagree with a school board's evaluation.[74] At the same time, a board may challenge a parental request for an independent evaluation in an administrative hearing, and if it turns out that the board's evaluation was appropriate, the parent(s) are not entitled to have an independent evaluation at public expense.[75]

Appropriate Placement

Although the IDEA requires school boards to provide a continuum of alternative placements for each student with a disability,[76] the statute offers little guidance in defining what may be considered appropriate. The IDEA's regulations indicate that an "appropriate education" consists of special education and related services that are provided in conformance with an IEP.[77] Even so, a precise definition of the term "appropriate" cannot be found in either the statute or its regulations. As such, it is necessary to turn to judicial interpretation for further guidance on the meaning of FAPE.

In *Board of Education of the Hendrick Hudson Central School District v. Rowley (Rowley)*,[78] the Supreme Court offered a minimal definition of a FAPE. *Rowley* arose when the parents of a kindergarten student in New York who was hearing impaired protested their school board's refusal to provide their daughter with a sign-language interpreter. Lower federal courts ordered the school board to provide the interpreter on the basis that an appropriate education was one that would have allowed the child to achieve at a level commensurate with that of her peers who were not disabled. The Supreme Court, in noting that the child was achieving passing marks and advancing from grade to grade without the sign-language interpreter, reversed the decision. The Court held that an appropriate education was one that was formulated in accordance with all of the IDEA's procedures and is "sufficient to confer some educational benefit"[79] on a child with a disability. Insofar as the child in *Rowley* received some educational benefit without the sign-language interpreter, the Court was convinced that educators were not required to provide one even though she might have achieved at a higher level with the services.

Rowley establishes a minimum standard of what constitutes a FAPE under federal law. Yet, individual states, such as North Carolina,[80] New Jersey,[81] Massachusetts,[82] Michigan,[83] and California[84] have upheld higher standards of appropriateness. In some of these cases, courts have specifically ruled that the higher state standards replaced the federal requirements since one of the essential elements of the IDEA is that special education programs must meet "the standards of the state educational agency."[85]

The *Rowley* standard has been further refined as courts have indicated that the "some educational benefit" criteria requires more than just minimal or trivial benefits.[86] Other courts have expanded the criteria by deciding that an educational benefit must be meaningful[87] or appreciable.[88] One court went so far as to maintain that a student's gains must be measurable to meet the *Rowley* criteria.[89] Regardless of which criteria are employed, subsequent case law has made it clear that under the IDEA's so-called "zero-reject" approach, each child with a disability must be served.[90]

Least Restrictive Environment

According to the IDEA, each student with a disability must be educated in the least restrictive environment (LRE).[91] In two cases, federal appellate courts directed school boards to place students with disabilities in regular settings as opposed to segregated special education classrooms. In these cases, the courts held that educators must consider a variety of factors when formulating a child's LRE.

In *Oberti v. Board of Education of the Borough of Clementon School District*,[92] a case from New Jersey, the Third Circuit adopted a two-part test for assessing compliance with the LRE requirement. The first element of the test is whether education in the regular classroom, with the use of supplementary aids and services, can be achieved satisfactorily. The second part of the test adds that if a placement outside of the regular classroom is necessary, educators must consider whether a child was mainstreamed (now referred to as full inclusion) to the maximum extent appropriate.[93]

> *Even with the focus on inclusion, not all students with disabilities must be placed in regular education classes. Courts have approved segregated settings where educators demonstrated that students with disabilities could not function in regular classrooms or would not benefit in such settings, even with supplementary aids and services.*

As summarized by the Ninth Circuit in *Sacramento City Unified School District Board of Education v. Rachel H.*,[94] a dispute from California, four factors must be addressed in making a placement: the educational benefits of placing a child with a disability in a regular classroom; the non-academic benefits of such a placement; the effect that the student's presence would have on the teacher and other children in the class; and the costs of an inclusionary placement. Educators must take all of these into account when placing a student with a disability.

Inherent in both of these cases is the principle that educators must make reasonable efforts to place students with disabilities in fully inclusive settings by providing them with supplementary aids and services to ensure success. Even with the focus on inclusion, not all students with disabilities must be placed in regular education classes. Courts have approved segregated settings where educators demonstrated that students with disabilities could not function in regular classrooms or would not benefit in such settings, even with supplementary aids and services.[95] The bottom line is that an inclusionary placement should be the setting of choice and a segregated setting should be contemplated only if an inclusionary placement has failed despite the best efforts of educators or there is overwhelming evidence that it is not feasible.

Private and Residential School Placements

The IDEA's preference for full inclusion is not feasible for all students. Even so, the IDEA does require school officials to offer a continuum of placement alternatives to meet the educational needs of children with disabilities.[96] In this regard, public school officials may be required to place a child in a non-public school when a board lacks an appropriate placement[97] such as when a student has a low incidence disability and there are not enough children with the same type of disability within the system to warrant the development of a program.[98] The courts have recognized that since smaller school boards probably cannot afford to develop specialized programs for small numbers of students, they must look elsewhere for placements.

A court may order a residential placement for a student with severe, profound, or multiple disabilities[99] if the child needs twenty-four hour per day programming or consistency between the school and home environments. Residential placements may also be necessary for a student with significant behavioral disorders[100] or who requires total immersion in an educational environment in order to progress.[101]

If a residential placement is required for purely educational reasons, its cost must be fully borne by a school board which cannot require parents to contribute toward its cost.[102] If a placement is made for other than educational reasons such as for medical or social purposes, then a school system may only be required to pay for the educational component of the residential setting[103] and may enter into a cost-share agreement with other agencies.

In the first of two cases that are illustrative of these issues, the Seventh Circuit affirmed that a mother in Illinois, who due to her failure to cooperate by refusing to give school officials a reasonable opportunity to evaluate her son, forfeited any claim to tuition reimbursement for unilaterally placing him in a private school.[104] The court rejected the mother's request because after her son was not permitted to return to a religiously affiliated school, she enrolled him in a private residential facility without first affording public school personnel the opportunity to evaluate his condition. Conversely, a federal trial court in Indiana awarded partial reimbursement where the private school chosen by the parents provided their son with an appropriate education but they failed to notify the school board in writing of their intent to enroll him there at public expense.[105] The court also commented that the board failed to provide the student with an appropriate program.

Extended School Year Programs

If a student with a disability requires an educational program that extends beyond the regular school year, it must be provided at public expense.[106] An extended school year program is generally necessary when a student regresses and the time it takes to recoup lost skills interferes with overall progress toward the attainment of the goals and objectives in a child's IEP.[107] Any regression that a student experiences must be greater than the regression that normally occurs during a school vacation. If a regression is minimal, an extended school year program is not required.[108]

Child Find

The IDEA regulations require states, through local educational agencies or school boards, to identify, locate, and evaluate all children with disabilities,[109] including those who attend religiously affiliated non-public schools,[110] regardless of the severity of their disabilities. The so-called "child find" activities under-

> *The IDEA regulations require states, through local educational agencies or school boards, to identify, locate, and evaluate all children with disabilities, including those who attend religiously affiliated non-public schools, regardless of the severity of their disabilities. The so-called "child find" activities undertaken to locate students in non-public schools who have disabilities must be comparable to those used to locate public school children with disabilities.*

taken to locate students in non-public schools who have disabilities must be comparable to those used to locate public school children with disabilities.[111] Further, the regulations require public school personnel to consult with appropriate private school representatives to determine how to carry out "child find" activities.[112]

The task of identifying children in need of services is generally delegated to individual school boards and their staffs. In order to locate children who may have disabilities, school board officials typically disseminate information about the services available to students with disabilities. This information is conveyed via newspaper articles, radio announcements, and advertisements on cable television. In addition, many school board officials may leave information pamphlets in locations frequented by parents of young children, such as pediatricians' offices, daycare centers, toy stores, and the like.

Insofar as early identification of children with disabilities is important, many school boards offer annual screenings for pre-school and kindergarten aged children.[113] While the kindergarten screening process is generally conducted as part of the normal kindergarten registration activities, educators usually set up special dates to screen pre-school aged children. Parents who suspect that their child has a disability can ask for a screening by appointment at any time during a school year.

Minimum Competency Tests

As many states have moved toward adopting high stakes testing in the call for greater accountability in the nation's classrooms, it is important to focus on legal issues surrounding minimum competency tests (MCTs). MCTs may be used either as a graduation requirement to assure that students receiving a diploma have a specified knowledge base or to identify students who have not achieved competency in basic skills and may require remedial instruction. The IDEA requires students with disabilities to participate in some form of state assessment.[114]

States clearly have the authority to develop and administer MCTs and to establish graduation requirements.[115] It is well settled that states may require students to pass MCTs to receive standard high school diplomas as long as they satisfy three primary guidelines. First, when these tests are used as a graduation requirement, they must not only be a valid, reliable measure of what has been taught but must also afford students sufficient notice that they must pass a MCT to receive a standard diploma.[116] Second, consistent with the non-discrimination standards in the IDEA's evaluation procedures,[117] MCTs may not be racially, linguistically, or ethnically discriminatory.[118] Third, in order to have students with disabilities take, and pass, a MCT before receiving a standard high school diploma,[119] along with sufficient notice of an examination, their IEPs should specifically identify areas in need of instruction so that they can be prepared for the test.

Similar to the accommodations that may be required for admissions testing under Section 504, students with disabilities taking MCTs may be entitled to modifications. School officials may be required to modify how a test is administered but are not obligated to change an examination's actual content or offer an alternate text. For example, a student who is blind should be given a braille version of the test while a child with a physical disability should be offered any necessary assistance writing or filling in the circles on a machine scored answer sheet. It is unlikely that a school board will be required to develop and administer a test with fewer items or easier items for a student with intellectual impairments.[120] Basically, school officials are obligated to provide modifications that will allow a student to take a test but do not need to modify the item content or compromise its validity. In such a situation, the Office of Civil Rights (OCR) entered an order in favor of a school board in Florida where educational officials rejected a parent's request that a proctor be permitted to read a MCT to her child. In observing that since the communication section of the examination was designed to test the student's reading and comprehension skills, OCR was of the view that school officials had the authority to reject the mother's request since granting it would have compromised the validity of the test.[121]

As part of a team, parents of children with disabilities are responsible for working with other members of an IEP team in determining the components of their child's IEP.[122] School officials should make parents aware of the general content of tests, where and how they are to be administered, and the purposes for which the results are to be used. Following an evaluation period, and prior to placement, a decision should be made regarding the appropriateness of including MCT material in a child's IEP. If an IEP team is satisfied that such content is inappropriate, the parent(s) may always appeal to an impartial hearing officer. Consequently, to the extent that educators routinely follow these practices, and keep parents involved, they are unlikely to face the threat of litigation involving proficiency testing of students with disabilities.

Related Services

School boards must provide related, or supportive, services to each child with a disability if they are necessary to help the student to benefit from special education.[123] The only limit on what can be a related service is that medical services are exempted unless they are specifically for diagnostic or evaluative purposes. One of the most controversial topics under the rubric of related services involves the distinction between medical and school health services. Procedures that must, by law, be performed by a licensed physician would be exempted medical services. Thus, psychiatric therapy would not be a related service since a psychiatrist is a licensed physician.

Many students with significant medical needs require round-the-clock nursing services. This type of service falls somewhere on the continuum between school health services and medical services. The Supreme Court first addressed this issue in *Irving Independent School District v. Tatro*,[124] when it held that a service such as catheterization that can be performed by a school nurse or a trained layperson is a required related service under the IDEA. More recently, the Court extended its rationale in *Cedar Rapids Community School District v. Garret F.*,[125] in finding that regardless of cost, a school board was required to provide, and pay for, a full-time nurse while a student was in school since his medical condition required constant nursing services.[126]

Assistive Technology

A potentially costly related service involves assistive technology. The 1990 revisions to the IDEA were the first to include definitions of assistive technology devices and services. The definitions of assistive technology devices[127] or services[128] were expanded and carried over into the 1997 IDEA Amendments. Comprehensive guidelines for implementing the assistive technology provisions of the IDEA were included in the final regulations for implementation of the 1997 Amendments.[129] Interestingly, assistive technology is not specifically included in either the definition of special education or related services. Assistive technology does fit within the definition of special education as specially designed instruction and within the definition of related services as a developmental, corrective, or supportive service. Yet, instead of including assistive technology within either of these two definitions, Congress chose to create assistive technology as a category separate from special education and related services. Accordingly, assistive technology can be considered to be either a special education service, a related service, or simply a supplementary aid or service. Regardless of which rubric they may be covered by, school boards are required to offer students with disabilities supplementary aids and services to allow them to be educated in the least restrictive environment.[130]

The IDEA[131] and its regulations[132] define an assistive technology device as any item, piece of equipment, or product system that is used to increase, maintain, or improve the functional capabilities of a student with a disability. These devices may include commercially available, modified, or customized equipment. An assistive technology service is further defined as any service that is designed to directly assist an individual with a disability in the selection, acquisition, or use of an assistive technology device. [133] This requires an evaluation of a student's needs including a functional evaluation of the child's customary environment; considering whether to purchase, lease, or otherwise provide for the acquisition of the assistive technology device; selecting, designing, fitting, customizing, adapting, applying, maintaining, repairing, or replacing the assistive technology device; coordinating and using other therapies, interventions, or services with assistive technology devices such as those associated with existing education and rehabilitation programs; training or providing technical assistance for the student or his or her family; and making training and technical assistance available to professionals who provide education or rehabilitation services as well as to employers or other individuals who offer services to the student with disabilities.

As indicated above, assistive technology may be provided as a special education service, a related service, or as a supplementary aid and/or service. Assistive technology is required when it is necessary for a student to receive a FAPE under the *Rowley* standard. Further, assistive technology may allow many students with disabilities to benefit from education in less restrictive settings and so may also be required under the IDEA's least restrictive environment provision.

A child's IEP team is required to consider whether a student requires assistive technology devices and services in order to receive an appropriate education.[134] Even so, no provisions direct a team to document its discussion of a student's assistive technology needs and whether they are or may be required. If a team determines that assistive technology is required, this must be written into a child's IEP.

School board officials are required to ensure that assistive technology devices and services are made available to a child if either or both are required as part of the student's special education, related services, or supplementary aids and services.[135] Additionally, the use of school-provided assistive technology devices is required in a student's home if an IEP team decides that the child needs access to assistive technology in order to receive a FAPE.[136]

In explanatory material accompanying the 1999 regulations, the Department of Education made it clear that school boards are not required to provide personal devices, such as eyeglasses, hearing aids, and/or braces, that a student would require regardless of whether the child attended school.[137] The Department also clarified its position in explaining that students with disabilities are entitled to access to any general technology that is available to peers who are not disabled. If a student with a disability requires an accommodation in order to use general technology, it must be provided.[138]

Remedies

If a school board fails to provide a student with a disability with a FAPE, the IDEA authorizes the courts to grant appropriate relief.[139] Frequently, the courts order school officials to provide specified special education and related services. However, as discussed below in the section on tuition reimbursement, if parents unilaterally obtain the necessary services at their own expense, a court may direct a school board to reimburse them for all legitimate expenses.

Procedural Due Process

Subject to the discussion below in the section on complaints, the IDEA's extensive due process procedures do not apply to students who attend religiously affiliated non-public schools. In public school settings, if parents disagree with any of a school board's actions regarding a proposed IEP or any aspect of a FAPE, they may seek mediation[140] or can invoke their right to a due process hearing[141] which must be presided over by a fair and impartial third-party decision maker.[142] A party that is not satisfied with the final result of administrative proceedings may appeal to the state or federal courts.[143] Before doing so, an aggrieved party must exhaust all administrative remedies prior to resorting to judicial review unless it is futile to do so. While an administrative or judicial action is pending, pursuant to the IDEA's so-called stay-put provisions which require a child to remain in his or her then current placement, school board officials may not change the student's placement without parental consent,[144] the hearing officer's order,[145] or a judicial decree.[146]

The IDEA empowers the courts to review the record of administrative proceedings, hear additional evidence, and "grant such relief as the court determines is appropriate"[147] based on the preponderance of evidence standard. At the same time, the Supreme Court has cautioned judges not to substitute their views of proper educational methodology for that of competent school authorities.[148] To the extent that the IDEA does not contain a statute of limitations for filing suit, courts must borrow one from analogous state statutes.[149]

The 1997 Amendments to the IDEA called for the resolution of disputes through mediation as an alternative to an adversarial proceeding.[150] Insofar as mediation is voluntary, it may not be used to deny or delay a parent's right to an administrative hearing.

The IDEA is not the exclusive avenue through which parents may enforce the rights of their child with a disability. The IDEA specifically stipulates that none of its provisions can be interpreted as restricting or limiting the rights, procedures, and remedies available under the Constitution, Section 504, or other federal statutes protecting the rights of students with disabilities.[151] Litigation is often initiated under Section 504, the ADA, and Section 1983 of the Civil Rights Act of 1871[152] in addition to the IDEA.

Damages

Courts generally have not imposed punitive damages on school authorities for failing to provide a FAPE to a child with a disability.[153] Similarly, general damages awards for "pain and suffering" have not been prevalent.[154] Recent litigation indicates that this may be changing.[155] Courts have remarked that monetary damages may be available under other statutes, such as Section 504, if parents can show that school officials intentionally discriminated against their child or egregiously disregarded the student's rights.[156] The operative word here is "intentionally." If school officials act in good faith but their efforts fall short of meeting statutory requirements, they should be immune from damages.

Tuition Reimbursement

Sometimes parents who are dissatisfied with a placement unilaterally enroll their child in a non-public school and seek to recover tuition expenses. The Supreme Court has ruled that parents are entitled to tuition reimbursement if they can show that a school board failed to offer a FAPE and that their chosen placement in a non-public school is appropriate.[157] The Court reasoned that awarding reimbursement simply requires a school board to pay retroactively the costs it should have been paying all along. The Court subsequently found that parents are entitled to reimbursement even if their chosen placement is not in a state approved facility as long as it provided an otherwise appropriate education.[158] Even so, when parents unilaterally place their children, they do so at their own financial risk because they are not entitled to reimbursement if school officials can show that they offered, and could provide, an appropriate educational placement. Parents are also entitled to reimbursement for unilaterally obtained related services if they can demonstrate that a school board failed to provide the needed services.[159]

Compensatory Services

Tuition reimbursement is likely to be of little use to parents who are unable to place their child unilaterally in a non-public school because they cannot afford to pay for tuition. When parents cannot afford to make a unilateral placement, their child may remain in an inappropriate setting while the dispute winds its way through due process hearings and judicial proceedings. In such a situation, a court may award additional educational services and prospective relief to compensate the parents and child for the loss of appropriate educational services.

The courts have pointed out that compensatory services, like reimbursement, compensate a student for a school board's failure to provide a FAPE. The rationale behind an award of compensatory services is that an appropriate remedy should not be available only to students whose parents can afford to provide them with an alternate educational placement while litigation is pending.[160] Generally, compensatory services are provided for a period of time equal to that for which the child was denied services[161] and may be granted even after a student has passed the ceiling age for eligibility under the IDEA.[162] As with tuition reimbursement, awards of compensatory educational services are granted only when a hearing officer or court has ascertained that a board failed to provide an appropriate placement.

Attorney Fees

It almost goes without saying that litigation can cost a great deal. Many parents, after prevailing in court against a school board reasonably expect to be reimbursed for their expenses in safeguarding the educational rights of their children. Parents argue that they achieve hollow victories when they prevail but are left with burdensome legal bills.

In 1984, the Supreme Court held that recovery of legal expenses was not available under the IDEA.[163] Two years later, Congress responded by amending the IDEA with the passage of the Handicapped Children's Protection Act (HCPA).[164] The HCPA gave courts the power to award reasonable attorney fees to parents who prevailed against school boards in actions or proceedings brought pursuant to the IDEA. An award must be based on the prevailing rates in the community in which the case arose. Under the HCPA, a court may determine what is a reasonable amount of time spent preparing and arguing a case. An award may be limited if a school board made a settlement offer more than ten days before the proceedings began that was equal to or more favorable than the final relief obtained.[165] Further, a court may reduce an award if it finds that parents unreasonably protracted the dispute,[166] an attorney's hourly rate was excessive,[167] or the time spent and legal services furnished were excessive in light of the issues.[168] The Act does not permit parents who are attorneys to recover fees for representing their own children.[169] The HCPA was made retroactive to July 4, 1984, the day before the Supreme Court declared that attorney fees were unavailable under the IDEA.

Discipline

Perhaps the most controversial legal issue in special education concerns disciplinary sanctions and students with disabilities.[170] Yet, until its 1997 Amendments were adopted, the IDEA did not make a direct reference to discipline. Disciplining students with disabilities is highly sensitive since it pits the duty of administrators to maintain order, discipline, and a safe environment against the rights of each child to receive a FAPE in the LRE. Even though most will agree that the power of school officials to maintain discipline should not be frustrated, it must be understood that a student should not be denied the rights accorded by the IDEA if misconduct is a manifestation of the child's disability.

School officials may impose a disciplinary sanction on a student in special education as long as they follow procedures that do not deprive the child of his or her rights. To this end, educators may use normal disciplinary sanctions, including suspensions, with special education students by following usual procedures and providing customary due process.[171] Administrators face some restrictions when they intend to impose more drastic punishments such as expulsions or wish to change students' placements for disciplinary reasons. Basically, in these situations, the due process procedures in the IDEA replace the normal due process protections.

Case law makes it clear that although a student with a disability cannot be expelled for misconduct that is a manifestation of his or her disability, a child can be excluded if there is no relationship between the misconduct and disability.[172] While the Supreme Court's landmark decision in *Honig v. Doe*[173] supported the prohibition against expelling students for disability-related misconduct, it did permit them to be suspended for up to ten school days. During the ten-day cooling off period, school personnel may attempt to negotiate an alternative placement with a student's parents. If school officials are unsuccessful in negotiating an alternative placement with parents, and can show that a student is truly dangerous, they may obtain an injunction or order allowing them to exclude the child from school.

The 1997 Amendments, which codified case law since *Honig*, clarified many of the gaps in the statute and implemented the most far-reaching changes to the IDEA since it was enacted. The IDEA now contains specific requirements and provisions for disciplining students with disabilities.[174] The regulations explicitly state that the unilateral removal of a student with a disability from the child's current educational placement for more than ten consecutive school days constitutes an impermissible change of placement.[175]

In a major change, the IDEA increases the authority of educators to deal with students with disabilities who possess weapons or drugs.[176] Under these provisions, educators may transfer a student with a disability to an interim alternative placement for up to forty-five school days for possession of a weapon or possession, use, sale, or solicitation of drugs on school property or at a school function.[177] School officials may also order a change in placement to an interim alternative setting if this sanction is used for students who are not disabled under similar circumstances.[178]

When a student with a disability is moved to an alternative placement, educators must conduct a functional behavioral assessment and implement a behavioral intervention plan for the child if one is not already in place.[179] If a behavioral intervention plan was in place when the child misbehaved, the IEP team must review the plan and its implementation in order to make any necessary modifications.[180] Should a parent disagree with the alternative placement and request a hearing, consistent with the IDEA's stay-put provision, the student must remain in the alternative setting.[181] Once the forty-five day period expires, educators must return the student to his or her prior educational placement[182] unless they can demonstrate that it is dangerous to do so.[183]

The amended IDEA expands the authority of hearing officers to order interim alternative placements of up to forty-five school days after an expedited due process hearing.[184] Previously, under *Honig*, educators could not impose such a change unless they had a court order. Even with this change, educators bear the burden of proving that keeping a student in the then current placement is substantially likely to result in injury to the child or others.[185] Still, school officials must demonstrate that they took reasonable measures to minimize that risk in the student's current placement.[186]

The IDEA requires an interim alternative placement to permit a student to continue to progress in the general education curriculum where he or she will still receive necessary services as outlined in his or her IEP.[187] Additionally, educators must provide services and modifications designed to prevent the misbehavior from recurring in the student's program.[188]

For the first time, the amended IDEA establishes procedures to evaluate whether misconduct is related to a student's disability.[189] The IDEA calls for this judgment to be made by the team that developed the student's IEP[190] within ten school days of when it chose to take disciplinary action.[191] At the so-called manifestation determination, a team must consider evaluative and diagnostic information, observations of the student, and the child's IEP and placement.[192] In evaluating whether misconduct is a manifestation of a disability, a team should examine whether a child's disability impaired his or her ability to understand the impact and consequences of the misbehavior along with whether the disability impaired the student's ability to control the behavior.[193] If, in making a determination, an IEP team is convinced that there were deficiencies in a student's IEP, its implementation, or the child's placement, it must order immediate steps to be taken to remedy the shortcomings.[194]

If an IEP team is convinced that a student's misbehavior is not a manifestation of his or her disability, then the child may be disciplined in the same manner as any child who is not disabled.[195] The disciplinary options available to educators do not forbid expulsion if it is the usual sanction for the misbehavior in question. A parent may challenge the result of a manifestation determination by requesting an expedited due process hearing.[196]

Another important change clarifies whether school officials can discontinue educational services for a student who is properly expelled for misconduct that is not disability-related. This provision codified existing policy from the United States Department of Education which ordered the delivery of educational services in this situation and effectively reversed a controversial decision from Virginia wherein the Fourth Circuit held that no such requirement existed under the IDEA.[197] The revised IDEA makes it clear that a FAPE must be made available to all students with disabilities including those who have been expelled from school.[198] In other words, even if a student with a disability has been expelled in accord with the IDEA's provisions, the child must be provided with services that will allow him or her to progress in the general education curriculum and achieve the goals of his or her IEP.[199]

It is important to keep in mind that a student with a disability can still be suspended for up to ten school days as long as this penalty can be imposed on a child who is not disabled.[200] Even so, under such a circumstance, school officials must conduct a functional behavioral assessment, if they have not already done so, and must address the student's misbehavior.[201] The regulations do not require officials to provide services to a child who has been suspended for ten days or less.[202] Of course, nothing prohibits school officials from providing services.

The courts have disagreed over the treatment of a student who has yet to be assessed for special education but claims to be covered by the IDEA. School officials must now provide the IDEA's protections to a student if they knew that the child was disabled before the misbehavior occurred.[203] School officials are considered to have this knowledge if a parent expresses concern that his or her child may need special education or makes a request for an evaluation. Educators may also be considered to be on notice of a child's disability based on a student's prior behavioral and academic history and/or concerns expressed by teachers.[204] An exception exists if educators already conducted an evaluation and decided that a student was not disabled.[205] If a parent requests an evaluation during the time when a student is subject to disciplinary sanctions, it must be conducted in an expedited manner.[206] Consistent with the IDEA's stay-put provision, until an expedited evaluation is completed, a student remains in the placement deemed appropriate by educators.[207] If an evaluation team decides that a child is disabled, school officials must provide the student with special education services.[208]

A final change in the discipline provisions explains that the IDEA cannot be interpreted as prohibiting school officials from reporting a crime committed by a student with a disability to the proper authorities or impeding law enforcement and judicial authorities from carrying out their responsibilities.[209] When school officials do report a crime, they must furnish a student's special education and disciplinary records to the appropriate authorities[210] to the extent that this is permitted under the Family Educational Rights and Privacy Act.[211]

V. The IDEA and Catholic Schools

Rather than engage in a discussion of the lengthy and complex history of litigation involving the acceptable parameters of aid to non-public schools under the Establishment Clause of the First Amendment,[212] suffice it to say that since the Supreme Court first enunciated the Child Benefit test,[213] which permits a variety of forms of aid to children in non-public schools, it has had a checkered history.[214] Moreover, virtually all litigation involving the Establishment Clause has been examined in light of the tripartite test enunciated by the Supreme Court in *Lemon v. Kurtzman*.[215] Under this seemingly ubiquitous standard:

> *Every analysis in this area must begin with consideration of the cumulative criteria developed by the Court over many years. Three such tests may be gleaned from our cases. First, the statute must have a secular legislative purpose; second, its principal or primary effect must be one that neither advances nor inhibits religion; finally, the statute must not foster "an excessive government entanglement with religion."*[216]

Perhaps the nadir of the Child Benefit Test occurred in 1985 when, in *Aguilar v. Felton*,[217] the Supreme Court banned the on-site delivery of remedial Title I[218] services in religiously affiliated non-public schools. The Court struck down a program in New York City even in the absence of any allegation of misconduct or misappropriation of public funds based on the fear that having public school educators provide services in religious schools might have created "excessive entanglement" between the government and religion. Consequently, since school boards still had to provide services at public schools or neutral sites, many students who attended religiously affiliated non-public schools were denied equal educational opportunities under Title I.[219]

Fortunately, from the point of view of those who are interested in Catholic and other religiously affiliated non-public schools, the landscape with regard to state aid to K-12 education began to evolve[220] in 1993 when the Supreme Court revitalized the Child Benefit test in *Zobrest v. Catalina Foothills School District (Zobrest)*.[221] In *Zobrest*, the Court ruled that the Establishment Clause did not bar a public school district in Arizona from providing the on-site delivery of the services of a sign language interpreter for a student who attended a Roman Catholic high school. The Court reasoned that since the interpreter was essentially a conduit through whom information passed, the on-site delivery of such assistance did not violate the Establishment Clause. Four years later, in *Agostini v. Felton*,[222] the Court virtually lifted the ban against the on-site delivery of services to students who attended religiously affiliated non-public schools in New York City as long as appropriate safeguards were in place. Most recently, in *Mitchell v. Helms*,[223] a suit from Louisiana, the Supreme Court,[224] in a plurality opinion upheld the constitutionality of Chapter 2, now Title VI, of Title I of the Elementary and Secondary Education Act,[225] a far-reaching federal statute which permits the loan of state-owned instructional materials such as computers, slide projectors, television sets, tape recorders, maps, and globes to non-public schools.[226]

A major statutory change occurred in 1997 when congressional reauthorization of the IDEA included provisions clarifying the obligations of public school systems to provide special education and related services to students in non-public schools. Unfortunately, neither Congress nor the courts conclusively answered questions about the delivery of special education for children in religiously affiliated non-public schools. Regulatory modifications in 1999 created a dilemma because while, on the one hand, they make it clear that children in religious schools are entitled to receive some special education services, on the other hand, they contain funding restrictions that may actually mean that these students will receive fewer services[227] in the event that officials in public schools follow only the letter of the law and do not make additional services available to youngsters who are qualified.

VI. The 1997 IDEA Amendments and 1999 Regulations

The 1997 Amendments to the IDEA[228] and its accompanying regulations[229] unequivocally declare that students whose parents voluntarily enroll them in religiously affiliated non-public schools are entitled to some level of participation in special education. The revised IDEA permits the on-site delivery of special education for students with disabilities on the premises of "private" schools, including "parochial" or "sectarian" schools,[230] as long as appropriate safeguards are in place to avoid "excessive entanglement" between the government *qua* public school boards and religious institutions. It has long been settled that public school personnel can conduct diagnostic tests on-site in Catholic, and other non-public schools, to determine whether children are eligible for services in programs that are supported by public funds.[231]

In implementing the IDEA, the Department of Education released updated regulations, *Assistance to States for the Education of Children with Disabilities,* in March 1999. These regulations, which are discussed in the following pages, incorporate the statutory changes and offer additional guidance on carrying out the IDEA's requirements while borrowing from the pre-existing Education Department General Administrative Regulations (EDGAR regulations).[232] The EDGAR regulations require school systems to provide students in non-public schools with opportunities for equitable participation in federal programs.[233] More specifically, these regulations stand for the proposition that students in non-public schools are entitled to equal opportunities to participate in federal programs that are of comparable quality to those available to children in public schools.[234] In developing such programs, public school personnel must consult with representatives of the non-public schools to consider which students will be served, how their needs will be identified, what benefits they will receive, how the benefits will be delivered, and how the programs will be evaluated.[235] As might have been anticipated, the IDEA and its accompanying regulations have been subject to litigation, discussed below, over the delivery of special education to students in religiously affiliated non-public schools.

> *...these regulations stand for the proposition that students in non-public schools are entitled to equal opportunities to participate in federal programs that are of comparable quality to those available to children in public schools.*

Definition of a "Private" School

According to the regulations, public school boards must locate, identify, and evaluate all students with disabilities who attend "private schools" within their jurisdictions, including children who attend religiously affiliated schools.[236] As such, school boards must develop plans to permit these students to participate in programs carried out pursuant to the IDEA.[237] The regulation defines students in non-public schools as those whose parents have voluntarily enrolled them in such schools or facilities.[238] This definition does not include students whose school boards have placed them in private facilities at public expense in order to provide each of them with a FAPE.

Spending Limits

The IDEA sets a cap on the amount of money that a school board must spend in providing services to pupils in non-public schools.[239] The total is limited to a proportionate amount of the federal funds received based on the number of students in non-public schools in relation to the overall number of pupils in the district.[240] School boards are not prohibited from using state funds to offer more than the IDEA calls for since the regulation only establishes a minimum amount that they must spend on children who attend religiously affiliated non-public schools.[241]

Under the new regulations, IDEA funds cannot be used to benefit private religiously affiliated non-public schools in ways that would violate the Establishment Clause.[242] In other words, public funds cannot be used to offer impermissible aid to religious institutions by financing existing instructional programs, otherwise providing them with direct financial benefits such as money, or organizing classes based on students' religions or schools they attend.[243] Even so, the regulations allow boards to employ public school personnel in these non-public schools as long as they are not supplanting services that are normally provided by those institutions.[244] The regulations further permit boards to hire personnel from non-public schools to provide services outside of their regular hours of work as long as they are under the supervision and control of officials from the public schools.[245] Finally, equipment purchased with IDEA funds can only be used on-site in non-public schools for the benefit of students with disabilities.[246]

> *...equipment purchased with IDEA funds can only be used on-site in non-public schools for the benefit of students with disabilities.*

Comparable Services

The regulations point out that students who attend non-public schools may not necessarily be entitled to participate to the same level as they would have had they been enrolled in public schools.[247] Consistent with this approach, students in non-public schools lack a private right of action to file a lawsuit in order to seek to receive services.[248] The regulations give public school officials, after consultation with representatives from non-public schools, the authority to decide which students from non-public schools will be served, what services they will receive, and how the services will be delivered.[249] This same section of the regulation emphasizes that the consultation must give representatives from the non-public schools a genuine opportunity to express their views prior to any decision-making about the expenditure of funds. Public school officials have the final authority to decide which services will be provided to eligible students in non-public schools.

Students in non-public schools are entitled to receive services from personnel who meet the same standards as educators in public schools[250] even though they may receive a different amount from their peers in public schools[251] and have no right to the same amount of aid as if they were enrolled in public schools.[252] Insofar as students in non-public schools are not entitled to a FAPE unless they attend a public school,[253] the regulations do not require the development of an IEP. Instead, the regulations require school board officials to develop a services plan, similar to the one discussed under Section 504, describing the assistance that they will provide to a student.[254] A services plan must meet an IEP's content requirements and must be developed, reviewed, and revised in a manner consistent with the IEP process.[255]

On-Site Delivery of Services

The regulations reiterate that services may be offered on-site at religiously affiliated non-public schools.[256] Consequently, in order to differentiate between schools, the regulations specifically use the term "religious school" to reflect the fact that they are included within the statutory framework.[257]

If services are not offered on-site and students must be transported to alternate locations to receive them, school boards must provide transportation.[258] Under this provision, it is important to recognize that the cost of transportation may be included in calculating the minimum amount of federal funds that school boards must spend on students in non-public schools. School boards need not transport students between their homes and religious schools since they must only do so between sites during the school day.

Complaints

The IDEA's regulations specify that the procedural safeguards generally do not apply to complaints that a school board has failed to deliver services to students in non-public schools.[259] The due process provisions do apply to complaints that a board failed to comply with the child find requirements that are applicable to students in non-public schools[260] and to those pursuant to allegations arising in connection with state administration of special education.[261]

Litigation Involving Students in Non-Public Schools

As often as the IDEA has been litigated, it is surprising that so relatively few of the cases contested the delivery of special education for students whose parents voluntarily enrolled them in religiously affiliated non-public schools. As might have been anticipated, since approximately 85% of students in non-public schools attend religiously affiliated schools,[262] most of the litigation has centered on questions involving the Establishment Clause. Even though the recent statutory and regulatory changes address many of the issues that were already litigated, a brief review of the pre-Amendment cases sets the stage for disputes directly involving the 1997 IDEA Amendments.

Pre-Amendment Litigation

A major controversy that the 1997 IDEA Amendments seem to have resolved is whether school boards must provide special education on-site at a student's religiously-affiliated non-public school. In *Goodall v. Stafford County School Board*,[263] the Fourth Circuit initially held that a board in Virginia met its obligation under the IDEA by offering such services at a local public school rather than the Christian school that the student attended. Following *Zobrest*,[264] the Fourth Circuit affirmed its earlier judgment in *Goodall v. Stafford County School Board (Goodall)*[265] that the services did not have to be provided on-site.

Four other courts agreed with *Goodall*.[266] These courts generally ruled that school boards met their obligations under the IDEA when services were made available to children at public schools. Yet, not all courts agreed as others interpreted the regulations as requiring boards to provide students in non-public schools with services that were comparable in quality, scope, and opportunity to those offered to their peers in public schools.[267] Insofar as three of these cases, *K.R. v. Anderson Community School Corporation*,[268] *Russman v. Sobol*,[269] and

Fowler v. Unified School District[270] were appealed to the Supreme Court, they are discussed in the next section of this book.

If a school board does not provide services on-site, the question arises as to whether it can be required to offer transportation to students between non-public schools and the locations where they receive services.[271] Even though a regulation specifically addresses this question by declaring that transportation must be provided if students need it to benefit from or participate in the special education programs, litigation has ensued.[272]

In *Felter v. Cape Girardeau School District*,[273] a federal trial court in Missouri reasoned that a school board had to provide transportation for a student with visual and mobility impairments from the sidewalk in front of her religiously affiliated non-public school to the public school where she attended special education classes. Conversely, in *Donald B. v. Board of School Commissioners of Mobile County*,[274] a judgment that was issued shortly after the passage of the 1997 IDEA Amendments but which involved a situation that occurred prior to its enactment, the Eleventh Circuit found that a school board in Alabama was not required to transport a student who attended an Episcopalian school to a public school for speech therapy. Although acknowledging that transportation was a related service, the court concluded that it was unnecessary since the student could walk safely from one school site to the other. These cases can be reconciled because in *Donald B.* the student was able to access services without transportation while in *Felter* the child's disabilities prevented her from taking advantage of the services without transportation between sites.

Post-Amendment Litigation

As appeals in *K.R. v. Anderson Community School Corporation*,[275] *Russman v. Sobol*,[276] and *Fowler v. Unified School District*[277] were pending before the Supreme Court, Congress passed the 1997 IDEA Amendments. Subsequently, the Court vacated these cases and returned the disputes to the lower courts for reconsideration in light of the Amendments. On remand, the courts had to consider what the school boards had to do both prior to and after the adoption of the 1997 IDEA Amendments because even though the suits arose before the changes were passed, the students continued to need special education.

In *K.R. v. Anderson Community School Corporation (Anderson)*,[278] the Seventh Circuit originally denied the request of a student from Indiana for an instructional aide on-site in her Catholic school. On remand in *K.R. v. Anderson Community School Corporation*,[279] the Seventh Circuit affirmed that the 1997 IDEA Amendments did not require states and school boards to spend their money to ensure that students with disabilities who attend non-public schools would receive publicly-funded special education comparable with what is offered to children in public schools. Similarly, a federal trial court in Wisconsin, citing *Anderson*, asserted that a hearing impaired student whose parents enrolled him in a Christian school was not entitled to the services of a sign language interpreter.[280] In decreeing that the 1997 IDEA Amendments confirmed that an interpreter did not have to be provided on-site in the religious school, the court wrote that the local school board complied with the law by offering a FAPE at a public school. The court was of the view that when the parents rejected the public school placement which offered an appropriate education, they elected a lesser entitlement for their son.

In a case that was resolved prior to the enactment of the IDEA Amendments, the Tenth Circuit, in *Fowler v. Unified School District (Fowler)*,[281] indicated that a school board in Kansas was not required to provide a sign language interpreter on-site at a private non-sectarian school if doing so cost more than delivering a similar service at a public school. On remand, the Tenth Circuit asserted that since the 1997 IDEA Amendments were not applicable retroactively, its original judgment stood with respect to events that took place before they went into effect on June 4, 1997.[282] Conversely, as to actions after June 4, 1997, the court explained that the school board's sole obligation was to spend a proportionate amount of federal funds on students in non-public schools. The court remarked that the Amendments did not require states and local school boards to spend their own funds to provide special education for children whose parents voluntarily enrolled them in non-public schools. The court was satisfied that school boards merely had to make a proportionate amount of federal funds available to pay for the education of children who attended non-public schools.

In *Russman v. Sobol*,[283] the Second Circuit initially declared that if delivering special education services at a Roman Catholic school entailed significant additional costs, a board in New York would have complied with the IDEA by offering them at a local public school. On remand under the name of *Russman v. Mills*,[284] the court agreed that the 1997 IDEA Amendments did not require school boards to spend their own funds on students with disabilities whose parents voluntarily enrolled them in non-public schools. Instead, the court was of the opinion that school boards were only required to offer services that could be paid for with a proportionate amount of the federal IDEA funds. The court reiterated that the IDEA does not obligate boards to deliver on-site services to students with disabilities whose parents voluntarily enrolled them in non-public schools since the language of the Act is permissive rather than mandatory. On remand from the Second Circuit, a federal trial court in New York issued yet another judgment in this long-standing dispute over the rights of a student who was mentally retarded to receive special education services on-site at her Catholic school.[285] The court declared that the school board was not required to provide the student with the necessary services on-site because insofar as the provision of the requested services was permissive, rather than compulsory, under the 1997 version of the IDEA, school officials were free to act as they did.

In *Cefalu v. East Baton Rouge Parish School Board (Cefalu)*,[286] the Fifth Circuit initially held that a hearing-impaired student in a Catholic school in Louisiana was entitled to the on-site delivery of the assistance of a speech language interpreter if he could demonstrate that he had a genuine need for such aid. After withdrawing its original opinion in light of the passage of the 1997 IDEA Amendments, the court reversed itself and found that the board was not required to furnish the student with an interpreter since he rejected its offer of a FAPE at a public school.[287]

The first of three cases from the Eighth Circuit was a dispute from Missouri that was resolved shortly after the 1997 IDEA Amendments went into effect. Here, a student in a Catholic school was denied the on-site delivery of special education services because the court was satisfied that the local school board met its obligation by offering them at a public school. In *Foley v. Special School District of St. Louis County*,[288] the court affirmed its pre-Amendment decision but relied on the revised version of the IDEA since the child and her parents sought prospective relief. The court contended that under the amended IDEA, the student did not have an individual right to receive special education at a particular location.

In *Peter v. Wedl (Wedl)*,[289] the Eighth Circuit ruled that a child in a Christian school in Minnesota did not have a right to the on-site delivery of services by a full-time paraprofessional. Yet, since the school board had a long-standing policy and practice of providing services to students with disabilities at non-religious, non-public, and home schools, the court reasoned that the denial of similar services to a student in a religiously affiliated school amounted to religious discrimination. The court added that under *Agostini*, the board lacked a valid argument that it risked violating the Establishment Clause by delivering special education at the religious school. On remand under the name *Westendorp v. Independent School District No. 273 (Westendorp)*,[290] the trial court acknowledged that since the board violated the pre-Amendment version of the IDEA by refusing to provide the child with the services he needed unless he attended a public school, he was entitled to prospective relief. In other words, the court concluded that since school officials violated the child's rights under the IDEA, he was entitled to the services of a full-time paraprofessional for the next six years regardless of where he attended school.

The Eighth Circuit, in *Jasa v. Millard Public School District No. 17*,[291] found that under the 1997 IDEA Amendments, since parents from Nebraska who unilaterally placed their son in a private residential facility had no individual right to special education and related service, they lacked the right to a court order mandating the delivery of services at a particular location. The court ruled that the child, who was severely disabled and needed constant medical attention, was not entitled to receive special education services at the licensed nursing facility where he had been placed by his parents. Prior to being placed in the nursing facility, the student had received the requested services at home.

Issues in Need of Clarification

As significant as the litigation surrounding the IDEA has been, at least four important issues are in need of further clarification about the delivery of special education for children in Catholic schools: whether services must be provided to all students whose parents voluntarily enroll them in religious schools; whether public school officials have discretion over where and how services are delivered; whether boards must offer services to children whose parents voluntarily enroll them in religiously affiliated non-public schools; and, whether there are specific safeguards that public school administrators must put in place pursuant to the delivery of special education services to children in religious schools.

Children Enrolled in Catholic Schools

As noted earlier, the IDEA does not direct boards of education to serve all children in religiously affiliated non-public schools. Rather, the IDEA requires boards to spend a proportionate share of their federal funds on students who are enrolled in non-public schools.[292] As long as boards spend the minimum amount of federal funds on these pupils, they will have met their obligations under the IDEA, even if all eligible children are not served. Accordingly, it is conceivable that school boards could serve some, but not all of these students. For example, boards could choose to serve only students with mild to moderate disabilities in the more common categories but not those with low-incidence disabilities. Thus, boards can spend all of their proportionate share of federal funds on a select group of children in non-public schools and none on the rest of the students. Alternatively, boards may provide services to all students with disabilities who attend non-public schools but each would receive only a proportionate share of services. In the latter case, the share of services that children in non-public schools would receive is likely be much less than that received by similarly-situated students in public schools.[293] At the same time, the IDEA continues to require boards to locate and identify students with disabilities who are attending non-public schools.[294]

Delivery of Services

The regulations grant public school officials a great deal of latitude over where and how special education services are offered to children in non-public schools.[295] Although the 1997 IDEA Amendments incorporated *Agostini v. Felton's* holding that allows public school boards to provide the on-site delivery of certain federally funded services at religiously affiliated non-public schools, the Act does not mandate such delivery.[296] The latitude that educators have over the delivery of services presumably includes the location where they are offered. Even so, before acting, public school officials must consult with representatives from the non-public schools and give them the opportunity to express their views.[297]

Case law supports the notion that school boards have satisfied the IDEA once they offer a student with a disability a FAPE. Consequently, if parents reject the delivery of services offered at a public school, a board is under no legal obligation to deliver them in a non-public school. The fact that an individual right to services does not exist can be found in the regulation which declares that the due process provisions of the IDEA are unavailable to students in non-public schools.[298] The Tenth Circuit's analysis in *Fowler* also indicated that a school board merely had to make a proportionate share of federal funds available to students in non-public schools.

In choosing where and how special education services are provided to pupils in non-public schools, administrators must make sure that they do not discriminate against a particular class of non-public school students. In other words, as in *Wedl/Westendorp*, educators cannot refuse to provide on-site services to children in religious schools while offering them to peers in nonsectarian institutions.

If a school system does not offer the on-site delivery of services and children from religiously affiliated non-public schools must travel to other locations, boards may be required to provide transportation. Insofar as transportation is a related service under the IDEA, boards must provide it where it is necessary for students to benefit from special education.[299] School boards may also have to offer transportation between sites when students need it in order to access related services. Courts have held that transportation is necessary if students require it but can be dispensed with if they can safely access services without transportation.

Services Available

Pursuant to the IDEA and its regulations, students who attend religiously affiliated non-public schools do not have the right to the same level of services that they would have received had they been in public schools. Consistent with both *Anderson* and *Cefalu,* since individual students do not even have the right to receive any services at all, boards are under no obligation to provide any particular level of services.

School boards that offer services to students in non-public schools need not spend more on them than on children in public schools for similar services. In fact, students in non-public schools can receive lesser services than similarly-situated peers in public schools if the cost of delivery to the former is greater than the cost of delivering the same to the latter.[300] The regulations support this interpretation in stating that individual students in non-public schools do not have the right to the same level of services that they would have received in public schools.[301] At the same time, both the IDEA and the regulations indicate that boards may pay for services for students in non-public schools only up to an amount equal to the federal funds that they would have spent on them if they were enrolled in public schools.[302] As such, if boards offer services to students with disabilities in non-public schools, they may provide only a level of services to each student that can be paid for with the proportionate share of federal funds. The net result is that in such a situation, each student would be likely to receive a bare minimum of services.

> *...both the IDEA and the regulations indicate that boards may pay for services for students in non-public schools only up to an amount equal to the federal funds that they would have spent on them if they were enrolled in public schools.*

The regulations dictate that boards providing services to individual students must employ personnel who meet the same certification standards as their counterparts in the public schools.[303] The regulations add that students in non-public schools do not have the right to receive the same amount of services as their peers in the public schools.[304] Consequently, while public school officials have some discretion in limiting the kind and extent of the services that they offer to children who attend religiously affiliated non-public schools, once they commit to provide services, they must be of comparable quality.

Safeguards for the On-Site Delivery of Services

The Supreme Court, in *Aguilar v. Felton*,[305] decided that the New York City Board of Education (NYCBOE) violated the Establishment Clause by allowing teachers and counselors paid with Title I funds to enter religiously affiliated non-public schools, mostly Roman Catholic schools and Hebrew Day Academies, to provide services to students. The Court struck down the practice even though the NYCBOE had controls in place based on the Court's unfounded fear of excessive entanglement between educators in the public and the religiously affiliated non-public schools. Twelve years later, in *Agostini v. Felton*,[306] the Court took the extraordinary step of expressly repudiating *Aguilar* by dissolving the injunction that enforced its earlier judgment. In *Agostini*, the Court found that the NYCBOE, and, by extension, other school boards, could, if they wished, but were not required to, provide Title I services on-site in religious schools. Relying in large part on the fact that the NYCBOE spent over $100 million on computer-aided instruction, leasing sites and mobile instructional units, and transporting students to those locations since 1986, the Court agreed that since appropriate procedures were in place, the funds would have been better spent educating students.[307]

The guidelines adopted by the NYCBOE in *Agostini* are relevant to special educators for two important reasons. First, since both the IDEA and Title I are federal laws, they are likely to be interpreted in a similar fashion. Second, the last of twenty-five questions in a memorandum issued by the Secretary of Education Richard W. Reily and the Department of Education shortly after *Agostini* was resolved indicated that it applies to federal programs other than Title I. According to the Department of Education:

> Question 25: Does the Supreme Court's decision in *Agostini* apply to other federal education programs?

> Answer: The Supreme Court's decision dealt directly with the issue of the constitutionality of providing instructional services under Title I, Part A to programs in private schools. However, the implication of the Court's ruling is that there is no constitutional bar to public school employees providing

educational services in private schools under other Federal programs under similar circumstances.[308]

The fact that many, but not all, of the safeguards that the NYCBOE used are incorporated in the memorandum from the Department of Education should be instructive to those developing programs providing on-site delivery of special education to students who attend religiously affiliated non-public schools, even if, as noted earlier, the IDEA does not require them to do so.

The NYCBOE instituted safeguards for its personnel who worked in religious schools under Title I. First, only staff who volunteered to do so were eligible to serve as Title I personnel in religiously affiliated schools. Second, assignments were made without regard to the religious affiliations of the public employees, most of whom worked in schools not of their own faiths. Third, Title I staff were supervised by field personnel from the NYCBOE who made frequent unannounced visits on at least a monthly basis. Fourth, all religious symbols were removed from the classrooms and offices used in Title I programs. Fifth, as itinerants, most Title I staff ordinarily did not spend a full week in one location. Sixth, the Title I personnel were told to limit their discussions with classroom teachers and other staff in the religious schools to matters of mutual concern over the education of the Title I students.

Title I personnel were also given detailed instructions highlighting the secular nature and purpose of that law while explaining the importance of avoiding excessive entanglement. First, staff were reminded that, as public school employees, they were responsible only to their own supervisors. Second, public employees were told that they could instruct only students who were approved by their supervisors. Third, staff were warned not to engage in team teaching or other cooperative instructional methodologies with personnel from the religious schools. Fourth, public employees were forbidden from introducing any religious materials in their classrooms and work areas. Fifth, staff were told to avoid involvement in religious activities at the schools where they worked. Finally, public employees were reminded that all materials and equipment purchased with Title I funds were to be used solely in that program.

Clearly, these guidelines provide a way to maintain a healthy separation between public schools and religiously affiliated non-public schools. Unfortunately, in light of the changes in the IDEA and its regulations, even these safeguards may be for naught if public school officials stick to the letter of the law and do not expand the range of services available to children who attend Catholic schools.

VII. Recommendations for Catholic School Administrators

T he final substantive section of this book offers advice for educational leaders in Catholic schools who have, or are considering, special education programs.

General Guidelines

In working with all stakeholders to provide special education services for children whose parents would like them to attend Catholic schools, educators in both Catholic and public schools should keep the lines of communication open by:

1. **Working with parents:** Administrators who suspect that a child has a disability should notify parents of their concerns immediately; this can be done with a telephone call and with a follow-up note that can also be used as documentation. Decisions should be made with the parents regarding whether a child needs to be assessed for special education and who will conduct the evaluation if one is deemed necessary. The IDEA provides that public school personnel can make such an evaluation. At the same time, if they so choose, parents may prefer to have an evaluation completed privately at their

own expense. If parents choose to have their own evaluation, either as a first step, or if they challenge the assessment performed by public school personnel, they should keep in mind that this can be an expensive process.

2. **Working with public school officials:** If a thorough assessment reveals that a student has a disability, administrators in the child's Catholic school should contact public school officials to determine what services, if any, the child's home school board is willing, and able, to provide. As noted earlier, while public schools are required to spend a proportionate share of their federal funds on students with disabilities who attend Catholic schools, they are not obligated to provide all of the required services that a child may need. Decisions about who is to be served and what services are to be provided are to be made jointly by officials from the Catholic and public schools. It should also be kept in mind that a public school board has met its legal obligation to students in Catholic schools once it has committed a proportionate share of its federal funds to the education of these children. Insofar as public schools often lack sufficient funds to provide all of the necessary services adequately for their own students, most will be unable to do more than meet their legal obligations to students in Catholic schools. Further, Catholic school administrators may need to understand that public school officials are not trying to be difficult, they simply have fiscal constraints that place limits on their resources.

3. **Understanding the parents' dilemma:** Parents may be required to balance their desire for a religion-based education with their child's need for special education services. Deciding which school their child attends can be a very difficult choice for parents. Catholic school administrators should understand these competing needs and work with parents to make decisions that are best for the child. In this regard, Catholic school officials must make a realistic assessment of what they can and will be able to provide for each child.[309] A frank discussion about what a Catholic school may be able to offer should help parents to make the most appropriate decision. If parents eventually choose to place their child in a public school, Catholic school

officials must work with the parents and their colleagues in the public schools to help the student to make a smooth transition.

4. Being prepared to make modifications: As noted above in the materials on Section 504 and the IDEA, many students with disabilities can succeed in regular classroom settings in Catholic schools with modifications to the learning environment and assignments. Thus, Catholic school administrators should work with public school educators and evaluators as well as parents to design modifications that allow students to be successful in their schools.

5. Providing staff development: Good teachers are able to meet the needs of most students with mild to moderate disabilities. Even so, many good classroom teachers received little training in their own preparation programs for working with students with disabilities. Staff development programs can go a long way toward helping these teachers improve their skills so that they can better meet the needs of all students in their classrooms, not just a child or children with disabilities. Administrators in Catholic schools should contact local public school officials to see what professional development activities are being offered to their own staffs since most public schools are likely to be more than willing to allow teachers in Catholic schools to attend these sessions.

6. Examining class sizes: Although data about the effectiveness of class size are inconclusive, class sizes for students in special education classes need to be smaller than they were just a few years ago. Students in today's classrooms, in both public and Catholic schools, have many needs that require a great deal of individualized attention. Even the best of teachers cannot meet the needs of all students in a large class. Smaller classes are much more conducive to educating students with mild to moderate disabilities within a regular education setting.

7. Understanding that a student with disabilities has the same right to an education as his or her peers who are not disabled: Consistent with Church teachings generally, and the statements of the American bishops particularly, a major principle of the IDEA is that a student with a disability is, first and foremost, a human being who has the same rights as all children including the right to an appropriate education. This also means that each child has the same right to a religion-based education as other students if that is what his or her parents desire. To this end, Catholic educational leaders should offer as much tutoring and other special education assistance as is feasible to allow students with disabilities to remain in their schools. While many parents must currently make a difficult decision between a religion-based education and needed special education services, perhaps some day they will not be required to make such a draconian choice.

Reflections for Elementary Schools

Catholic schools neither exist in isolation nor do their students check their citizenship rights "at the schoolhouse gate."[310] Even so, it is not reasonable to assume that Catholic schools can meet the needs of all children with disabilities. As educational leaders in Catholic schools embark on the path of inclusion, they must do all they can to learn about serving students with disabilities in a Catholic school environment. Consistent with the IDEA, opportunities in Catholic schools should range from full-time placement in regular classes to self-contained classes to part-time programs with services provided in Catholic and public schools. The needs of special education students can also be met by supplementary aids including pull-out programs using special education teachers, paraprofessionals, nontraditional technologies, peer partnerships, cross age tutoring, and large print books.

The new way of looking at how Catholic schools meet the needs of all students, including those with disabilities, is a break from earlier prescriptions. Thus, from the outset, administrators in Catholic elementary (and secondary) schools should seek to comply with the following IDEA checklist in order to assure that all students with disabilities:

- have access to the general education curriculum,
- receive special education that is a service and not a place to which they are sent,
- have options to receive a broad range of services addressing their needs,

- receive the assistance of an IEP team that first considers a placement in a local school with appropriate aids and services,
- have a continuum of placement options,
- receive full access to procedural and substantive rights and ensure that their parents are informed and participate in the decision-making process,
- have programs that incorporate regular assessment strategies, and
- have opportunities for involvement with non-disabled peers.

This new paradigm creates a paradox for Catholic educators as it sets the tone for collaboration, inclusion, and doing the right thing for special needs children. However, educators in Catholic schools must be careful not to raise the hopes of parents too high because providing a fully inclusive placement for some children may be an insurmountable challenge.

Placing a focus on the needs of children with disabilities means that administrators in parish schools must provide leadership and support strategies in the shift from, in some instances, the non-existence of special education programs to full inclusion. Making such a change may be easier than it seems in Catholic schools because of the limitations of the size of bureaucracy in implementing programs and not being constrained by pre-existing or poor models.[311] Even though the IDEA challenges educators in Catholic schools to seek new ways to support the needs of all students, educators may have a prototype in Title I remedial programs in *Agostini v. Felton*. The challenge for Catholic educators is to set up strategic alliances, partnerships, and collaborative efforts with public school personnel and other agencies that help to develop a system-wide focus on improving teaching and learning, flexibility at the local level in tandem with clear accountability, more precisely targeting resources, and stronger partnerships between schools and communities.

The IDEA raises such key questions as which students will be identified and served, what services they will receive, and where they will be offered. In identifying which students are served, it is worth recalling that a public school board is only required to expend federal monies proportionate to the ratio of the number of children with disabilities in Catholic schools to the total number of such students in the district. Consequently, as administrators in Catholic schools consult with parents, they would be wise to inform them that their children may have to forgo services that they might otherwise have received had they attended public schools. Moreover, administrators from Catholic and public schools must consult over which services will be offered and/or which populations will be targeted. For example, this means that some dioceses may opt for speech pathology so that they may serve a broad group of students while others may have to settle for services in grades K-6 in an effort to provide early needs assessments. Additionally, who receives benefits may vary depending on the relationship that Catholic school administrators have established with local public school officials.

It goes without saying that parents are a child's best advocate. Together, if there is a question whether a child needs special education, parents and a Catholic school administrator or school counselor (if available) should set up an appointment with public school officials to discuss whether the child can be assessed. If it turns out that a child needs special education, then his or her parent(s) will have the opportunity to serve on the child's IEP team and help to shape the learning environment in which he or she will be educated. Depending on a child's needs, an IEP team should help school staff to identify the range, or continuum, of available services. Students with disabilities should be placed in special classes, separate schools, or removed from a regular educational environment only when the nature or severity of a disability is such that, even with the use of supplementary aids and services, their education cannot be satisfactorily achieved in an inclusive setting. Although it may be implausible to think that all students in Catholic schools will benefit from all possible options under the IDEA, they have a greater likelihood of availing themselves of some of these programs by having necessary interventions and services and providing opportunities for involvement with non-disabled peers.

As to how and where services can be provided, once again the Title I model provides some guidance. Under Title I, services can be delivered on-site in a Catholic school since they are for the child and not the school. Yet, even if an IEP team recommends that a child receive services in a Catholic school, nothing permanent can be built there nor any of the equipment be utilized for religious instruction or anything to do with worship. The Title I model offers interesting options to explore when seeking programs for students in Catholic schools. Among these choices are instructional services provided at a public school site, at other public and privately owned neutral sites, in mobile vans or portable units, with educational radio, television, or computer-assisted instruction, extended-day services, home tutoring, take-home computers, and interactive technology.

To the extent possible, the goal of the IDEA is for students with disabilities to enroll at schools they would ordinarily have attended. The "neighborhood school" approach, which is predicated on the belief that students with disabilities be educated in their own communities, surrounded by siblings and friends, to the maximum extent possible, is beneficial to all children. Such an approach would be logical if all parents who choose Catholic schools for their children could have special education services provided on-site. Until such time as states can provide special education services on-site in Catholic schools, educational leaders in Catholic schools must "render unto Caesar that which is Caesar's and to God that which is God's"[312] and do all that they can to provide an inclusive education for as many children with disabilities as is feasible.

In order to work toward full inclusion, educational leaders in Catholic schools should involve all stakeholders in a planning process to create a new delivery model for students with disabilities since this should ensure the best use of resources to realize the potential of each child. The belief that Catholic schools are the best place to encourage greater creativity and flexibility in the development of instructional designs for all children, including students with disabilities, seems to be the hope of parents who are depending on Catholic schools to help educate their children in a Christ-centered environment.

Recommendations for Catholic High Schools

Historically, Catholic high schools have worked hard to provide for individual differences among students despite a lack of funding and programs similar to those available to children who attend public schools. True to the mission of Catholic education, the dedication of administrators, teachers, and staffs along with the nurturing of the local school and parish communities have helped academically challenged students to experience success through classes and adjusted curricula geared to their ability. These efforts were evident long before students with disabilities became a focus of public concern and ultimately, the law.

In discussing special education in Catholic secondary schools, just as is the case with elementary schools, it is necessary to distinguish degrees of special education. All Catholic schools, not just secondary schools, should be able to incorporate some or all of the following strategies to assist students with learning disabilities and moderate physical and behavioral disabilities: buildings and facilities that are readily accessible to the disabled; special tutoring programs staffed with appropriately trained/certified personnel; assessment procedures to determine the needs of individual students; and/or classes geared to students with learning (and other) disabilities (content comparable with regular classes but employing teaching strategies designed to address special learning needs).

> *In seeking to provide better services for children with disabilities, Catholic school leaders should consider not only exploring possible partnerships with local public schools but should also form collaborative efforts with Catholic high schools in areas where several are close to one another.*

Specific accommodations for students in need of special education (many of which require minimal expenditures) should include individualized testing procedures such as additional time or oral testing; permitting tape-recording of class presentations; a buddy-system for note taking; outlines of class presentations for note taking; orientation programs for students to make them aware of their responsibilities to be of assistance to peers with special needs; and adapted/adjusted co-curricular activities for students' physical abilities

The number of students enrolled in Catholic schools with severe learning, physical, and behavioral disabilities is generally few. While it is beyond the scope of this book to attempt to determine why this is the case, it is the reality. In light of this reality, strategies employed to meet the needs of small numbers of students may differ dramatically from the strategies discussed herein. In seeking to provide better services for children with disabilities, Catholic school leaders should consider not only exploring possible partnerships with local public schools but should also form collaborative efforts with Catholic high schools in areas where several are close to one another. Collaborative efforts involving Catholic schools could take one of the following forms:

1. Each school in an area could assume responsibility for providing a particular specialized service. Students with a particular need could enroll in the specified high school or in their home high school and be transported for a portion of the day to avail themselves of that service.

2. One school in the area could service all the specialized needs and the other schools could contribute monetary and/or personnel resources to support the program.

3. On a regional basis, satellite schools strategically positioned in a geographical area could provide services for special needs students. These would be sponsored by the diocese or the state Catholic schools association.

4. Cooperatively sponsored committees comprised of school representatives could be formed on a local level to determine student needs and available resources.

5. On-going staff development opportunities should be offered for all school personnel to address special education issues in the Catholic high school.

6. The local conference of bishops could provide a resource specialist who focuses on special education issues in Catholic schools, communicates with local and state education agencies, and familiarizes parents with the rights of children with disabilities.

VIII. Conclusion

Recent statutory, regulatory, and judicial changes dealing with the delivery of special education in religiously affiliated non-public schools have left children in Catholic schools with the proverbial half of a loaf of bread. That is, while the law makes it clear that students in Catholic schools are entitled to special education, the funding restrictions may actually limit the amount of services that they receive on-site. Thus, it is imperative to ensure that stakeholders in Catholic education understand the parameters of the law of special education so that they can work together to ensure that all children, including students with disabilities, receive the best possible education that they need and deserve.

Endnotes

1. United States Conference of Catholic Bishops, *To Teach as Jesus Did: A Pastoral Message on Catholic Education* par. 99 (Washington, DC: United States Conference of Catholic Bishops, 1972), p. 27.

2. The bishops reaffirmed the principles of *To Teach as Jesus Did* in *In Support of Catholic Elementary and Secondary Schools* (United States Conference of Catholic Bishops, *In Support of Catholic Elementary and Secondary Schools* (Washington, DC: United States Conference of Catholic Bishops, 1990)).

3. This book uses the term "parents" to include parents and guardians.

4. Robert J. Kealey, *Balance Sheet for Catholic Elementary Schools: 1999 Income and Expenses,* Exhibit 29, Percentage of Schools Nationally with Students with Selected Disabilities (Washington, DC: NCEA, 2000), p. 33. Although it is beyond the scope of this book, it is interesting to note that this same report points out that 22% of the responding schools had programs for gifted students.

5. Available on line at http://www.nccbuscc.org/doctrine/disabilities.htm

6. *See also* United States Conference of Catholic Bishops, *The Catholic School on the Threshold of the Third Millennium, Congregation for Catholic Education* (Washington, DC: United States Conference of Catholic Bishops, 1997) p. 38 ("Finance is a source of further difficulties, which are felt more acutely in which no governmental aid is provided for non public schools. This places an unbearable financial burden on families . . . and constitutes a serious threat to the survival of the schools themselves. Moreover, such financial strain not only affects the recruiting and stability of teachers, but can also result in the exclusion from Catholic schools of those who cannot afford to pay, leading to a selection according to means which deprives the Catholic school of one of its distinguishing features, which is to be a school for all.")

7. For excellent overviews on the rights of children with disabilities who attend non-public schools, *see* Ralph D. Mawdsley, *Legal Problems of Religious and Private Schools, 4th ed.* (Dayton, OH: Education Law Association, 2000), pp.

198-203 (Section 504), pp. 243-250 (IDEA); Ralph D. Mawdsley, "Religious Schools and the IDEA: An Ongoing Controversy," *Education Law Reporter, Vol. 125, No. 2*, p. 595 (1998); Ralph D. Mawdsley, "On-Site IDEA Services in Private Schools," *Education Law Reporter, Vol. 121, No. 2*, p. 445 (1997). *See also* Nikki L. Schweinbeck, "Section 504 and Catholic Schools," *Catholic Education: A Journal of Inquiry and Practice, Vol. 4, No. 4*, p. 464 (2001); Mary Elizabeth Blackett, "Recommendations for Catholic School Administrators in Facilitating Special Education Services," *Catholic Education: A Journal of Inquiry and Practice, Vol. 4, No. 4*, p. 479 (2001).

8. 29 U.S.C. § 794. A third statute, the Americans with Disabilities Act (ADA), although similar to Section 504, is beyond the scope of this book because it specifically exempts religious institutions from the scope of its coverage. The ADA, 42 U.S.C. §§ 12101 *et seq.*, was adopted in 1990 to provide "a comprehensive national mandate for the elimination of discrimination against individuals with disabilities." 42 U.S.C. § 12101(b)(2). The ADA effectively extends the protections of section 504 to the private sector but has implications for public entities such as schools.

9. 20 U.S.C. §§ 1400 *et seq.* Initially enacted in 1975 as the Education for All Handicapped Children Act, the name of the law changed in 1990 to the Individuals with Disabilities Education Act to place primary emphasis on individuals. In order to avoid inconsistency, unless otherwise noted, this book uses the term "disabled," rather than "handicapped," along with the current title and/or acronym throughout, even for material that predates 1990.

10. The status of special education law remains in some flux. *See* Michael A. Fletcher, "Bush Administration Gears Up to Revamp Special Education," *Washington Post*, Oct. 5, 2001, A 3 (noting that the Bush administration is seeking some changes in the IDEA, especially with regard to funding). *See also* Erik W. Robeson, "Spending Plans Favor Title I, Special Education," *Education Week*, Oct. 17, 2001, pp. 23, 25 (indicating that Title I and special education would receive some of the largest increases in funding under proposed House and Senate appropriations bills).

11. 34 C.F.R. § 300.453(d).

12. 34 C.F.R. § 300.453(d).

13. Even though the IDEA and its regulations actually use the terms "private" and "parochial" schools, the authors prefer and typically refer to schools that are non-public and/or religiously affiliated non-public schools.

14. For earlier versions of some of the materials discussed herein, *see* Charles J. Russo & Allan G. Osborne, Jr., "The Legal Rights of American Students with Disabilities: An Overview," *Australia & New Zealand Journal of Law & Education, Vol. 3, No. 2*, p. 45 (1998). Charles J. Russo, Joseph D. Massucci, & Allan G. Osborne, Jr., "The Delivery of Special Education Services in Catholic Schools: One Hand Gives, the Other Hand Takes Away," *Catholic Education: A Journal of Inquiry and Practice, Vol. 3, No. 3*, p. 375 (2000).

15. 268 U.S. 510 (1925).

16. According to the National Center for Educational Statistics August 2001 report, more students (2,511,040) were enrolled in Catholic schools, p. 5, accounting for almost half (48.6%) of the non-public school population in the United States. *Private School Universe 2001* (Washington, DC: United States Department of Education, 2001), p. 3.

17. 347 U.S. 483 (1954).

18. *Id.* p. 493.

19. Stephen B. Thomas & Charles J. Russo, *Special Education: Issues & Implications for the '90s* (Topeka: National Organization on Legal Problems of Education, 1995) pp. 4-5. *See also* Allan G. Osborne, Jr, *Legal Issue in Special Education* (Boston: Allyn and Bacon, 1996), pp. 3-4.

20. Joseph Ballard, Bruce A. Ramirez, & Frederick J. Weintraub. *Special Education in America: Its Legal and Governmental Foundations* (Reston, VA: Council for Exceptional Children, 1982), p. 2.

21. House Report No. 332, 94ᵗʰ Congress (1975) p. 11.

22. 334 F. Supp. 1257 (E.D. Pa. 1971), 343 F. Supp. 279 (E.D. Pa. 1972).

23. 348 F. Supp. 866 (D.D.C. 1972).

24. 29 U.S.C. § 794(a).

25. In an interesting case, a federal trial court in Louisiana rejected the argument of a Catholic school, and the diocese, that while the school received federal financial assistance, it was not a recipient within the meaning of Section 504. As such, the court permitted parental claims that the school failed to accommodate their son's disability, attention deficit hyperactivity disorder, to proceed. *Dupre v. Roman Catholic Diocese of Houma-Thibodaux*, 1999 WL 694081 (E.D. La. 1999).

26. 34 C.F.R. § 104.39 Private education.
(A) A recipient that provides private elementary or secondary education may not, on the basis of handicap, exclude a qualified handicapped person if the person can, with minor adjustments, be provided an appropriate education, as defined in § 104.33(b)(1), within that recipient's program or activity.
(B) A recipient to which this section applies may not charge more for the provision of an appropriate education to handicapped persons than to nonhandicapped persons except to the extent that any additional charge is justified by a substantial increase in cost to the recipient.
(C) A recipient to which this section applies that provides special education shall do so in accordance with the provisions of §§ 104.35 and 104.36. Each recipient to which this section applies is subject to the provisions of §§ 104.34, 104.37, and 104.38.

27. *See Bob Jones Univ. v. United States*, 461 U.S. 574 (1983) (upholding the revocation of tax exempt status on the ground that it constitutes a federal benefit). *See also Hunt v. St. Peter Sch.*, 963 F. Supp. 843 (W.D. Mo. 1997) (directing a Catholic school to comply with Section 504 because it received federal funds through Title I and other federal programs).

28. 29 U.S.C. § 706(7)(B). The regulations further define physical or mental impairments as including:

(A) Any physiological disorder or condition, cosmetic disfigurement, or anatomical loss affecting one or more of the following body systems: neurological; musculoskeletal; special sense organs; respiratory, including speech organs; cardiovascular; reproductive, digestive, genito-urinary; hemic and lymphatic; skin; and endocrine; or

(B) Any mental or psychological disorder, such as mental retardation, organic brain syndrome, emotional or mental illness, and specific learning disorders. 45 C.F.R. § 84.3(j)(2)(i), 34 C.F.R. § 104.3(j)(2)(i). Further, a note accompanying this list indicates that it merely provides examples of the types of impairments that are covered; it is not meant to be exhaustive.

29. An individual who is regarded as having an impairment has:

(A) A physical or mental impairment that does not substantially limit major life activities but that is treated by a recipient as constituting such a limitation;

(B) A physical or mental impairment that substantially limits major life activities only as a result of the attitudes of others toward such impairment; or

(C) None of the impairments . . . but is treated by a recipient as having such an impairment. 45 C.F.R. § 84.3(j)(2)(iv), 34 C.F.R. § 104.3(j)(2)(iv).

30. According to the regulations, "'Major life activities means functions such as caring for one's self, performing manual tasks, walking, seeing, hearing, speaking, breathing, learning, and working." 45 C.F.R. § 84.3(j)(2)(i).

31. 45 C.F.R. § 84.3(k)(2).

32. See 34 C.F.R. § 104.39. "A recipient that operates a private elementary or secondary education program may not, on the basis of handicap, exclude a qualified handicapped person from such program if the person can, with minor adjustments, be provided with an appropriate education, as defined within [34 C.F.R. §] 104.33(b)(1), within the recipient's program."

33. See Hunt. v. St. Peter Sch., 963 F. Supp. 843 (W.D. Mo. 1997) (holding that a Catholic school did not violate Section 504 in not maintaining a mandatory "scent-free" environment for a child with severe asthma because she was not otherwise qualified to participate in its educational program; the court was satisfied that the school's voluntary "scent-free" policy met Section 504's "minor adjustment" standard).

34. Sullivan v. Vallejo City Unified Sch. Dist., 731 F. Supp. 947 (E.D. Cal 1990).

35. Thomas v. Davidson Academy, 846 F. Supp. 611 (M.D. Tenn. 1994).

36. Barnes v. Converse College, 436 F. Supp. (D.S.C. 1977) (ordering a college to provide an interpreter, at its own expense, for a hearing impaired teacher who was admitted to a summer program).

37. At least one court has held that Section 504 does not require affirmative efforts to overcome a student's disability but only prohibits discrimination on the basis of the disability. See Lyons v. Smith, 829 F. Supp. 414 (D.D.C. 1993).

38. Another major difference between the laws is that the federal government provides public schools with direct federal financial assistance to help fund programs under the IDEA but does not offer any financial incentives to aid institutions, public and non-public, as they seek to comply with the dictates of Section 504.

39. *See, e.g., Guckenberger v. Boston Univ.*, 8 F. Supp.2d 82 (D. Mass. 1998) (upholding the decision of university officials not to permit students with learning disabilities to make course substitutions for its foreign language requirement where other means of accommodating them were available).

40. *Southeastern Community College v. Davis*, 442 U.S. 397, 410 (1979) (upholding a nursing program's refusal to admit a student with a learning disability). *See also Alexander v. Choate*, 469 U.S. 287 (1985) (ruling that Section 504 only requires reasonable modifications, not substantial changes), *Wynne v. Tufts Univ. Sch. of Med.*, 976 F.2d 791 (1st Cir. 1992), *cert. denied* 507 U.S. 1030 (1993) (holding that a medical school did not have to offer an alternative form of an examination to a student with a learning disability since this would have been a substantial alteration in the program and would have lowered standards).

41. *Davis, id.* p. 412. *See also William S. v. Gill*, 572 F. Supp. 509 (E.D. Ill. 1983) (deciding that Section 504 did not require a school board to send a student to a private residential facility if the cost of doing so far exceeded that of having him remain in a public school).

42. *See School Bd. of Nassau County v. Arline*, 480 U.S. 273, 287-88 (1987) (setting forth the criteria for determining whether, under Section 504, a teacher with tuberculosis posed a significant health risk to the school community). *See also Doe v. Woodford County*, 213 F.3d 921 (6th Cir. 2000) (affirming that school officials in Kentucky could keep a student off of a junior varsity basketball team while they assessed whether his being a carrier of the hepatitis B virus presented a direct threat to the health and safety of others).

43. 34 C.F.R. § 104.4(b)(3).

44. 34 C.F.R. § 104.34(c).

45. 34 C.F.R. § 104.39(b).

46. 34 C.F.R. § 104.36.

47. 34 C.F.R. § 104.5.

48. 34 C.F.R. § 104.35 Evaluation and placement.

(A) Preplacement evaluation - A recipient that operates a public elementary or secondary education program or activity shall conduct an evaluation in accordance with the requirements of paragraph (b) of this section of any person who, because of handicap, needs or is believed to need special education or related services before taking any action with respect to the initial placement of the person in regular or special education and any subsequent significant change in placement.

(B) Evaluation procedures - A recipient to which this subpart applies shall establish standards and procedures for the evaluation and placement of persons who, because of handicap, need or are believed to need special education or related services which ensure that:

(1) Tests and other evaluation materials have been validated for the specific purpose for which they are used and are administered by trained personnel in conformance with the instructions provided by their producer;

(2) Tests and other evaluation materials include those tailored to assess

specific areas of educational need and not merely those which are designed to provide a single general intelligence quotient; and

(3) Tests are selected and administered so as best to ensure that, when a test is administered to a student with impaired sensory, manual, or speaking skills, the test results accurately reflect the student's aptitude or achievement level or whatever other factor the test purports to measure, rather than reflecting the student's impaired sensory, manual, or speaking skills (except where those skills are the factors that the test purports to measure).

(C) Placement procedures - In interpreting evaluation data and in making placement decisions, a recipient shall:

(1) Draw upon information from a variety of sources, including aptitude and achievement tests, teacher recommendations, physical condition, social or cultural background, and adaptive behavior;

(2) Establish procedures to ensure that information obtained from all such sources is documented and carefully considered;

(3) Ensure that the placement decision is made by a group of persons, including persons knowledgeable about the child, the meaning of the evaluation data, and the placement options, and;

(4) Ensure that the placement decision is made in conformity with § 104.34.

(D) Re-evaluation - A recipient to which this section applies shall establish procedures, in accordance with paragraph (b) of this section, for periodic re-evaluation of students who have been provided special education and related services. A re-evaluation procedure consistent with the Education for the Handicapped Act is one means of meeting this requirement.

49. See St. Johnsbury Academy v. D.H., 240 F.3d 163 (1st Cir. 2001) (holding that a private independent school was not required to admit a student who could not meet its requirement of performing at a fifth grade level since she was not otherwise qualified; the court noted that Section 504 does not require an educational institution to lower its standards).

50. See, e.g., Tips v. Regents of Texas Tech Univ., 921 F. Supp. 1515 (N.D. Tex. 1996) ruling that the inability to conceptually organize material on a doctoral comprehensive examination was not a disability within the meaning of Section 504.

51. See, e.g., Argen v. New York State Bd. of Law Examiners, 860 F. Supp. 84 (W.D.N.Y. 1994) (deciding that an applicant failed to prove by a preponderance of the evidence that he was learning disabled).

52. See, e.g., Price v. National Bd. of Med. Examiners, 966 F. Supp. 419 (S.D. W.Va. 1997) (finding that three students with attention deficit hyperactivity disorder failed to show any substantial limitation on learning ability that would require additional time and a separate room for taking an examination) and Gonzalez v. National Bd. of Med. Examiners, 60 F. Supp.2d 703 (E.D. Mich. 1999) (upholding the Board's refusal to grant extra time for examinations for a student whose scores on several other examinations were in the average to superior range).

53. *See, e.g., Begay v. Hodel*, 730 F. Supp. 1001 (D. Ariz. 1990).

54. *Sullivan v. Vallejo City Unified Sch. Dist.*, 731 F. Supp. 947 (E.D. Cal. 1990).

55. *Eva N. v. Brock*, 741 F. Supp. 626 (E.D. Ky. 1990); *Kohl v. Woodhaven Learning Ctr.*, 865 F.2d 930 (8th Cir. 1989).

56. The IDEA is still sometimes referred to as P.L. 94-142, indicating that it was the one-hundred and forty-second piece of legislation introduced during the Ninety-Fourth Congress.

57. 20 U.S.C. § 1412(a)(1)(B)(i)(ii).

58. 20 U.S.C. § 1401 (3) offers the following definition:
Child with a disability:
In general, the term "child with a disability" means a child:
(A) With mental retardation, hearing impairments (including deafness), speech or language impairments, visual impairments (including blindness), serious emotional disturbance (hereinafter referred to as "emotional disturbance"), orthopedic impairments, autism, traumatic brain injury, other health impairments, or specific learning disabilities; and
(B) Who, by reason thereof, needs special education and related services.
Child aged 3 through 9:
The term "child with a disability" for a child aged 3 through 9 may, at the discretion of the State and the local educational agency, include a child:
(A) Experiencing developmental delays, as defined by the State and as measured by appropriate diagnostic instruments and procedures, in one or more of the following areas: physical development, cognitive development, communication development, social or emotional development, or adaptive development; and
(B) Who, by reason thereof, needs special education and related services.

59. *Id.* § 1401 (3)(A) (ii).

60. 20 U.S.C. § 1401 (8) Free appropriate public education:
The term "free appropriate public education" means special education and related services that:
(A) Have been provided at public expense, under public supervision and direction, and without charge;
(B) Meet the standards of the State educational agency;
(C) Include an appropriate preschool, elementary, or secondary school education in the State involved; and
(D) Are provided in conformity with the individualized education program required under section 1414(d) of this title.

61. 20 U.S.C. §§ 1401 (11), 1414 (d*). See* 34 C.F.R. §§ 300.340-350 for additional details on IEPs.

62. 20 U.S.C. § 1414(d)(1)(A).

63. 20 U.S.C. § 1401(3)(A)(ii).

64. This book uses the term "special education" to include both special education and related services.

65. 20 U.S.C. § 1415.

66. 29 U.S.C. § 1232g.

67. 34 C.F.R. §§ 300.560-577.
68. 20 U.S.C. §§ 1414(d)(1)(B)(i) and 1414(f).
69. 20 U.S.C. § 1414(a)(1)(C).
70. 20 U.S.C. § 1415(b)(3).
71. 20 U.S.C. § 1415(b)(3)(A).
72. 20 U.S.C. § 1414(d)(4)(A).
73. 20 U.S.C. § 1414(a)(2)(A).
74. 20 U.S.C. § 1415(b)(1).
75. 34 C.F.R. § 300.502(b).
76. 34 C.F.R. § 300.551. In practice, the range of options moves from full inclusion in regular education to inclusion with supplementary assistance such as an aide to partial inclusion to partial resource room placement to an individualized placement in a resource room to a special day school to hospital or homebound instruction to a residential placement. Typically, the first four options are offered in a child's local school.
77. 34 C.F.R. § 300.8.
78. 458 U.S. 176 (1982).
79. *Id.* p. 200.
80. *Harrell v. Wilson County Sch.*, 293 S.E.2d 687 (N.C. Ct. App. 1982); *Burke County Bd. of Educ. v. Denton*, 895 F.2d 973 (4th Cir. 1990).
81. *Geis v. Board of Educ. of Parsippany-Troy Hills*, 774 F.2d 575 (3rd Cir. 1985).
82. *David D. v. Dartmouth Sch. Comm.*, 775 F.2d 411 (1st Cir. 1985); *Roland M. v. Concord Sch. Comm.*, 910 F.2d 983 (1st Cir. 1990).
83. *Nelson v. Southfield Pub. Sch.*, 384 N.W.2d 423 (Mich. Ct. App. 1986); *Barwacz v. Michigan Dep't of Educ.*, 681 F. Supp. 427 (W.D. Mich. 1988).
84. *Pink v. Mt. Diablo Unified Sch. Dist.*, 738 F. Supp. 345 (N.D. Cal. 1990).
85. 20 U.S.C. § 1401(a)(18)(B).
86. *Hall v. Vance County Bd. of Educ.*, 774 F.2d 629 (4th Cir. 1985); *Carter v. Florence County Sch. Dist. Four*, 950 F.2d 156 (4th Cir. 1991), *aff'd on other grounds*, 510 U.S. 7 (1993).
87. *Board of Educ. of East Windsor Reg'l Sch. Dist. v. Diamond*, 808 F.2d 987 (3rd Cir. 1986); *Polk v. Susquehanna Intermediate Unit 16*, 853 F.2d 171 (3rd Cir. 1988).
88. *Chris C. v. Gwinnett County Sch. Dist.*, 780 F. Supp. 804 (N.D. Ga. 1991).
89. *J.S.K. v. Hendry County Sch. Bd.*, 941 F.2d 1563 (11th Cir. 1991).
90. Perhaps the seminal case on "zero-reject" is *Timothy W. v. Rochester, N.H., Sch. Dist.*, 875 F.2d 954 (1st Cir. 1989), *cert. denied* 493 U.S. 983 (1989) (holding that since there was no requirement in the IDEA that a child with a disability must necessarily benefit from special education, a board was required to pay for the residential placement of a student with multiple disabilities who was also profoundly mentally retarded).
91. 20 U.S.C. § 1412(5)(A).
92. 995 F.2d 1204 (3rd Cir. 1993).
93. This test was originally proposed in *Daniel R.R. v. State Bd. of Educ.*, 874 F.2d 1036 (5th Cir. 1989).

94. 14 F.3d 1398 (9th Cir. 1994).

95. *See, e.g., Clyde K. v. Puyallup Sch. Dist. No. 3*, 35 F.3d 1396 (9th Cir. 1994); *Capistrano Unified Sch. Dist. v. Wartenberg*, 59 F.3d 884 (9th Cir. 1995).

96. 34 C.F.R. § 300.551(a).

97. 20 U.S.C. § 1412(a)(10)(B), 34 C.F.R. § 300.349.

98. *See, e.g., Colin K. v. Schmidt*, 715 F.2d 1 (1st Cir. 1983).

99. *Gladys J. v. Pearland Indep. Sch. Dist.*, 520 F. Supp. 869 (S.D. Tex. 1981).

100. *Chris D. v. Montgomery County Bd. of Educ.*, 743 F. Supp. 1524 (M.D. Ala. 1990).

101. *Abrahamson v. Hershman*, 701 F.2d F.2d F.2d 223 (1st Cir. 1983)

102. *Parks v. Pavkovic*, 753 F.2d 1397 (7th Cir.1985)

103. *McKenzie v. Jefferson*, EHLR 554:338 (D.D.C. 1983).

104. *Patricia P. v. Board of Educ. of Oak Park and River Forest High Sch. Dist. No. 200*, 203 F.3d 462 (7th Cir. 2000).

105. *Nein v. Greater Clark County Sch. Corp.*, 95 F. Supp.2d 961 (S.D. Ind. 2000).

106. 34 C.F.R. § 300.309.

107. *Armstrong v. Kline*, 476 F. Supp. 583 (E.D. Pa. 1979), *remanded sub nom. Battle v. Commonwealth of Pa.*, 629 F.2d 269 (3d Cir. 1980), *on remand* 513 F. Supp. 425 (E.D. Pa. 1981), *Cordery v. Euckert*, 917 F.2d 1460 (6th Cir. 1990).

108. *Anderson v. Thompson*, 658 F.2d 1205 (7th Cir. 1981).

109. 34 C.F.R. § 300.125.

110. 34 C.F.R. § 451(a).

111. *Id.*

112. 34 C.F.R. § 451(b).

113. Early identification and assessment is listed as a related service at 20 U.S.C. § 1401(22).

114. 20 U.S.C. § 1412(a)(17), 34 C.F.R. § 300.138.

115. Ohio, for example, permits IEP teams to justify a student with a disability's being excused from taking a proficiency test; the same provision forbids school officials from prohibiting such a child from taking a proficiency test. O.R.C. § 3301.0711(c)(1). Yet, Ohio law has created an ambiguity since the statute is unclear as to exact nature of the assessment that a child in a special education placement must complete. Presumably, the form of assessment must be spelled out in a child's IEP.

116. *Debra P. v. Turlington*, 730 F.2d 1405 (11th Cir. 1984). *See also Anderson v. Banks*, 520 F. Supp. 472 (S.D. Ga. 1981), *modified*, 540 F. Supp. 761 (S.D. Ga. 1982), *appeal dismissed sub. nom., Johnson v. Sikes*, 730 F.2d 644 (11th Cir. 1984) (upholding the use of the California Achievement Test (CAT) where school officials were able to provide empirical data to support a claim of instructional validity in a district that had operated under de jure segregation); *Board of Educ. of Northport-East Northport Union Free Sch. Dist. v. Ambach*, 458 N.Y.S.2d 680 (N.Y. App. Div. 1982) (upholding minimum competency testing without having to prove instructional validity because, unlike *Debra P.* and *Anderson*, no prior de jure race discrimination occurred).

117. 20 U.S.C. § 1412(a)(6)(b), 34 C.F.R. § 300.532.
118. *Debra P. v. Turlington*, 730 F.2d 1405 (11th Cir. 1984).
119. *Debra P., id.* (striking down testing on the basis that thirteen-month notice was insufficient); *but see Brookhart v. Illinois State Bd. of Educ.*, 697 F.2d 179 (7th Cir. 1983) (although unwilling to define adequate notice in terms of a specific number of years, the court ruled that by changing a diploma require-ment and by providing only one and one-half years notice for students to prepare for a minimum competency test, school officials deprived failing students of both property and liberty rights; further, the court stipulated that a school board must ensure that students with disabilities be exposed to most of the test material or show that a well-informed decision was made not to pursue an MCT-based program); *Anderson v. Banks*, 520 F. Supp. 472 (S.D. Ga. 1981), *modified* 540 F. Supp. 761 (S.D. Ga. 1982) (holding that twenty-four month notice was sufficient due to the presumed general applicability of the CAT, the availability of remedial alternatives, and the ease of coordinating activities in a single district).
120. *Brookhart v. Illinois State Bd. of Educ.*, 697 F.2d 179 (7th Cir. 1983).
121. 28 I.D.E.L.R. 1002 (1998).
122. 20 U.S.C. § 1414(d)(1)(B)(i), 300 C.F.R. § 300.345.
123. 20 U.S.C. § 1401(a)(22). The IDEA specifically lists developmental, support-ive, or corrective services such as transportation, speech pathology, audiology, psychological services, physical therapy, occupational therapy, recreation (in-cluding therapeutic recreation), social work services, counseling services (in-cluding rehabilitation counseling), medical services (for diagnostic or evalu-ative purposes only), and early identification and assessment as related services.
124. 468 U.S. 883 (1984).
125. 526 U.S. 66 (1999).
126. For a discussion of this case and its implications, *see* Charles J. Russo *"Cedar Rapids Community School District v. Garret F.:* School Districts Must Pay for Nursing Services Under the IDEA," *School Business Affairs, Vol. 65, No. 6,* p. 35 (1999).
127. 20 U.S.C. § 1401(a)(1).
128. 20 U.S.C. § 1401(a)(2).
129. 34 C.F.R. §§ 300 *et seq.*
130. *Oberti v. Board of Educ. of the Borough of Clementon Sch. Dist.*, 995 F.2d 1204 (3d Cir. 1993).
131. 20 U.S.C. § 1401(1).
132. 34 C.F.R. § 300.5.
133. 20 U.S.C. § 1401(2), 34 C.F.R. § 300.6.
134. 34 C.F.R. § 300.346.
135. 34 C.F.R. § 300.308.
136. *Id.*
137. *64 Fed. Reg.* 12406 *et seq.* at 12591 (March 12, 1999).
138. *Id.* at 12540.

139. 20 U.S.C. § 1415(e)(2).

140. 34 C.F.R. § 300.506.

141. 20 U.S.C. §§ 1415(f)(g). *See also* 34 C.F.R. §§ 300.500-517 for the regulations relating to procedural safeguards.

142. 34 C.F.R. § 300.508.

143. 20 U.S.C. § 1415(i)(2)(B).

144. 20 U.S.C. § 1415(j).

145. 20 U.S.C. § 1415(k)(2).

146. *Honig v. Doe*, 484 U.S. 305 (1988).

147. 20 U.S.C. § 1415(i)(2)(B).

148. *Board of Educ. of Hendrick Hudson Cent. Sch. Dist. v. Rowley*, 458 U.S. 176, 208 (1982). According to the Court, "[w]e previously have cautioned that courts lack the "specialized knowledge and experience" necessary to resolve "persistent and difficult questions of educational policy . . . . Therefore, once a court determines that the requirements of the Act have been met, questions of methodology are for resolution by the States [through school officials.]" (Internal citations omitted).

149. *See, e.g., Providence Sch. Dep't v. Ana C.*, 108 F.3d 1 (1st Cir. 1997) (applying Rhode Island's Administrative Code), *Scokin v. Texas*, 723 F.2d 432 (5th Cir. 1984) (applying Texas law).

150. 20 U.S.C. § 1415(e).

151. 20 U.S.C. § 1415(l).

152. 42 U.S.C. § 1983.

153. *See, e.g., Marvin H. v. Austin Indep. Sch. Dist.*, 714 F.2d 1348 (5th Cir. 1983).

154. *See, e.g., Ft. Zumwalt Sch. Dist. v. Missouri State Bd. of Educ.*, 865 F. Supp. 604 (E.D. Mo. 1994).

155. For a discussion of damages in special education, *see* Allan G. Osborne, Jr. & Charles J. Russo, "Are Damages an Available Remedy When a School District Fails to Provide an Appropriate Education under IDEA?" *Education Law Reporter, Vol. 152, No. 1*, p. 1 (2001).

156. *See, e.g., W.B. v. Matula*, 67 F.3d 484 (3rd Cir. 1995); *Whitehead v. School Dist. for Hillsborough County*, 918 F. Supp. 1515 (M.D. Fla. 1996).

157. *Burlington Sch. Comm. v. Department of Educ., Commonwealth of Mass.*, 471 U.S. 359 (1985).

158. *Florence County Sch. Dist. Four v. Carter*, 510 U.S. 7 (1993).

159. Courts have ordered districts to reimburse parents for the costs of counseling or psychotherapy where they proved that the services were necessary for their children to benefit from special education. *See, e.g., Gary A. v. New Trier High Sch. Dist. No. 203*, 796 F.2d 940 (7th Cir. 1986); *Straube v. Florida Union Free Sch. Dist.*, 801 F. Supp. 1164 (S.D.N.Y. 1992).

160. *See, e.g., Lester H. v. Gilhool*, 916 F.2d 865 (3rd Cir. 1990); *Todd D. v. Andrews*, 933 F.2d 1576 (11th Cir. 1991); *Manchester Sch. Dist. v. Christopher B.*, 807 F. Supp. 860 (D.N.H. 1992).

161. *See, e.g., Valerie J. v. Derry Cooperative Sch. Dist.*, 771 F. Supp. 483 (D.N.H.

1991); *Big Beaver Falls Area Sch. Dist. v. Jackson*, 624 A.2d 806 (Pa. Commw. Ct. 1993).

162. *See, e.g., Pihl v. Massachusetts Dep't of Educ.*, 9 F.3d 184 (1st Cir. 1993); *Jones v. Schneider*, 896 F. Supp. 488 (D.V.I. 1995).

163. *Smith v. Robinson*, 468 U.S. 992 (1984).

164. 20 U.S.C. § 1415(e)(4)(B), 34 C.F.R. § 300.513.

165. *See, e.g., Virginia M.C. v. Corrigan-Camden Indep. Sch. Dist.*, 909 F. Supp. 1023 (E.D. Tex. 1995).

166. *Howie v. Tippecanoe Sch. Corp.*,734 F. Supp. 1485 (N.D. Ind. 1990).

167. *Beard v. Teska*, 31 F.3d 942 (10th Cir. 1994).

168. *Mr. D. v. Glocester Sch. Comm.*, 711 F. Supp. 66 (D.R.I. 1989); *Hall v. Detroit Pub. Sch.*, 823 F. Supp. 1377 (E.D. Mich. 1993).

169. *See Woodside v. School Dist. of Philadelphia Bd. of Educ.*, 248 F.3d 129 (3rd Cir. 2001); *Erickson v. Board of Educ. of Baltimore County*, 162 F.3d 289 (4th Cir. 1998).

170. For a lengthier discussion of this topic, *see* Charles J. Russo & Allan G. Osborne, Jr., "An American Dilemma: Disciplining Students with Disabilities," *Education Law Journal, Vol. 1, No. 1*, p. 13 (2000).

171. The procedures for disciplining students in regular education were spelled out for the first time in *Goss v. Lopez*, 419 U.S. 565 (1975).

172. *See, e.g., S-1 v. Turlington*, 635 F.2d 342 (5th Cir. 1981).

173. 484 U.S. 305 (1988).

174. 20 U.S.C. § § 1415(i)(j)(k)(l).

175. 34 C.F.R. § 300.519(a).

176. 34 C.F.R. § 300.520(a)(2).

177. 20 U.S.C. § 1415(k)(1), 34 C.F.R. § 300.520.

178. 34 C.F.R. § 300.520(a)(2).

179. 34 C.F.R. § 300.520(b)(1)(I).

180. 34 C.F.R. § 300.520(b)(1)(ii).

181. 34 C.F.R. § 300.526(a).

182. 34 C.F.R. § 300.526(b).

183. 34 C.F.R. § 300.526(c).

184. 20 U.S.C. § 1415(k)(2), 34 C.F.R. § 300.521, 34 C.F.R. § 300.528.

185. 34 C.F.R. § 300.521(a).

186. 34 C.F.R. § 300.521(c).

187. 34 C.F.R. § 300.522(b)(1).

188. 34 C.F.R. § 300.522(b)(2).

189. 20 U.S.C. § 1415(k)(4).

190. 34 C.F.R. § 300.523(b).

191. 34 C.F.R. § 300.523(a)(2).

192. 34 C.F.R. § 300.523(c)(1).

193. 34 C.F.R. § 300.523(c)(2).

194. 34 C.F.R. § 300.523(f).

195. 20 U.S.C. § 1415(k)(5), 34 C.F.R. § 300.524.

196. 34 C.F.R. § 300.525.

197. *Commonwealth of Va. Dep't of Educ. v. Riley*, 106 F.3d 559 (4th Cir. 1997).

198. 20 U.S.C. § 1412(a)(1)(A).

199. 34 C.F.R. § 300.121(d)(2)(i).

200. 34 C.F.R. § 300.121(d)(1).

201. 20 U.S.C. § 1415(k)(1)(B).

202. 34 C.F.R. § 300.121(d).

203. 20 U.S.C. § 1415(k)(8).

204. 34 C.F.R. § 300.527(b).

205. 34 C.F.R. § 300.527(d).

206. 34 C.F.R. § 300.527(d)(2)(i).

207. 34 C.F.R. § 300.527(d)(2)(ii).

208. 34 C.F.R. § 300.527(d)(2)(iii).

209. 20 U.S.C. § 1415(k)(9), 34 C.F.R. § 300.529.

210. 34 C.F.R. § 300.529(b)(1).

211. 20 U.S.C. § 1232g.

212. In relevant portion, the First Amendment declares that "Congress shall make no law respecting an establishment of religion, or prohibiting the free exercise thereof . . . . "

213. *Everson v. Board of Educ.*, 330 U.S. 1 (1947 (upholding a statute from New Jersey that authorized the reimbursement of parents for the cost of transportation associated with sending their children to non-public schools).

214. For a review of the major cases involving government aid to religiously affiliated non-public schools, *see* Charles J. Russo, Gerald M. Cattaro, & Allan G. Osborne, Jr. "State Aid to Religiously Affiliated Non-Public Schools: An Emerging Trend or Same Old Same Old?" *Journal of Research in Christian Education, Vol. 8, No. 2*, p. 267 (1999).

215. 403 U.S. 602 (1971).

216. *Id.* at 612-613 (internal citations omitted). When addressing entanglement and state aid to institutions that are religiously affiliated, Chief Justice Burger noted that the Court took three additional factors into consideration: "[w]e must examine the character and purposes of the institutions that are benefitted, the nature of the aid that the State provides, and the resulting relationship between the government and religious authority." *Lemon v. Kurtzman*, 403 U.S. 602, 615 (1971).

217. 473 U.S. 402 (1985).

218. Title I of the Elementary and Secondary Education Act, 20 U.S.C. §§ 2701 *et seq.*

219. As a result of *Aguilar*, one researcher estimated that 30% of all eligible Title I students in religiously affiliated non-public schools were deprived of educational benefits that they were entitled to receive under Title I. *See* Ralph D. Mawdsley & Charles J. Russo, "Supreme Court Upholds Religious Liberty: Educational Implications," *Education Law Reporter, Vol. 84, No. 3*, pp. 877, 893 at note 141 (1993).

220. The metamorphosis actually began in *Witters v. Washington Dep't of Servs. for the Blind*, 474 U.S. 481 (1986) (holding that the First Amendment did not

preclude a state from extending aid under a vocational rehabilitation assistance program to a blind student who chose to study at a Christian college to become a pastor, missionary, or youth director on the basis that the help was generally available without regard for the sectarian or non-sectarian nature of the institution), *rehearing denied, Witters v. Washington Dep't of Servs. for the Blind,* 475 U.S. 1091 (1986). The Supreme Court of Washington, in *Witters v. State Comm'n for the Blind,* 771 P.2d 1119 (Wash. 1989), *cert. denied sub nom. Witters v. Washington Dep't of Servs. for the Blind,* 493 U.S. 850 (1989), subsequently found that language in the state constitution prohibited the use of public funds for religious instruction.

221. 509 U.S. 1 (1993).
222. 521 U.S. 203 (1997).
223. *Helms v. Cody,* 856 F. Supp. 1102 (E.D. La. 1994), *aff'd in part, rev'd in part sub nom. Helms v. Picard,* 151 F.3d 347 (5th Cir. 1998), *cert. granted sub nom. Mitchell v. Helms,* 527 U.S. 1114 (1999), *rev'd* 527 U.S. 1002 (2000), *on remand,* 229 F.3d 467 (5th Cir. 2000).
224. For a discussion of this case and its implications, *see* Ralph D. Mawdsley & Charles J. Russo, "Religious Schools and Government Assistance: What is Acceptable After Helms?" *Education Law Reporter, Vol. 151, No. 2,* p. 373 (2001).
225. Chapter 2 of Title I [now Title VI] of the Elementary and Secondary Education Act, 20 U.S.C.§§ 7301-7373.
226. In the part of the case most relevant to special education, the Fifth Circuit, in *Helms v. Picard,* 151 F.3d 347 (5th Cir. 1998), reversed an earlier trial court judgment and upheld a state law that permitted the on-site delivery of special education services to children who attended Catholic schools; the court also affirmed the constitutionality of a state law which provided that these same children were entitled to free transportation to and from school. These parts of the case were not appealed to the Supreme Court.
227. For a discussion of these issues, *see* Charles J. Russo, Joseph D. Massucci, & Allan G. Osborne, Jr., "The Delivery of Special Education Services in Catholic Schools. One Hand Gives, the Other Hand Takes Away," *Catholic Education: A Journal of Inquiry and Practice, Vol. 3, No. 3,* p. 375 (2000).
228. 20 U.S.C. § 1412(a)(10).
229. 34 C.F.R. § 451.
230. 20 U.S.C. § 1412(a)(10)(A)(i)(II)).
231. *See Meek v. Pittenger,* 421 U.S. 349 (1975), *Wolman v. Walter,* 433 U.S. 229 (1977).
232. Education Department General Administrative Regulations, 34 C.F.R. §§ 76.1 *et seq.*
233. 34 C.F.R. § 76.651(a)(1).
234. 34 C.F.R. § 76.654(a).
235. 34 C.F.R. § 76.652(a)(1)-(5).
236. 34 C.F.R. § 300.451

237. 34 C.F.R. § 300.452

238. 34 C.F.R. § 300.450.

239. 34 C.F.R. § 300.453.

240. 20 U.S.C. § 1412(a)(10)(A)(i)(I)).

241. 34 C.F.R. § 453(d).

242. 34 C.F.R. §§ 300.459, 34 C.F.R. §§ 76.658.

243. 34 C.F.R. §§ 300.458.

244. 34 C.F.R. §§ 300.460.

245. 34 C.F.R. §§ 300.461.

246. 34 C.F.R. §§ 300.462.

247. 34 C.F.R. § 455(a)(3).

248. 34 C.F.R. § 454(a)(1).

249. 34 C.F.R. § 300.454(b).

250. 34 C.F.R. § 300.455(a)(1).

251. 34 C.F.R. § 300.455(a)(2).

252. 34 C.F.R. § 300.455(a)(3).

253. A local school board is not required ". . . to pay for the cost of education, including special education and related services of a child with a disability at a private school or facility if [it] made a FAPE available to the child and the parents elected to place the child in a private school or facility." 34 C.F.R. § 300.403(a)

254. 34 C.F.R. § 300.455(b)(1).

255. 34 C.F.R. § 300.455(b)(2).

256. 34 C.F.R. § 300.456(a).

257. 34 C.F.R. § 300.451(a).

258. 34 C.F.R. § 300.456(b).

259. 34 C.F.R. § 300.457(a).

260. 34 C.F.R. § 300.457(b).

261. 34 C.F.R. § 300.457(c).

262. National Center for Educational Statistics, *Digest of Educational Statistics* (Washington, DC: United States Department of Education, 1997), Table 59, p. 70.

263. 930 F.2d 363 (4th Cir. 1991).

264. *Zobrest v. Catalina Foothills Sch. Dist.*, 509 U.S. 1 (1993).

265. 60 F.3d 168 (4th Cir. 1995).

266. *Tribble v. Montgomery*, 798 F. Supp. 668 (M.D. Ala. 1992); *Foley v. Special Sch. Dist. of St. Louis County*, 927 F. Supp. 1214 (E.D. Mo. 1996), *motion for reconsideration denied* 968 F. Supp. 481 (E.D. Mo. 1997), *aff'd* 153 F.3d 863 (8th Cir. 1998); *K.R. v. Anderson Community Sch. Corp.*, 81 F.3d 673 (7th Cir. 1996), *vacated and remanded* 117 S. Ct. 2502 (1997) (mem.), *on remand*, 125 F.3d 1017 (7th Cir. 1997); *Cefalu v. East Baton Rouge Parish Sch. Bd.*, 117 F.3d 231 (5th Cir. 1997), previous decision at 103 F.3d 393 (5th Cir. 1997) withdrawn.

267. *Natchez-Adams Sch. Dist. v. Searing*, 1996, 918 F. Supp. 1028 (S.D. Miss. 1996).

268. 81 F.3d 673 (7th Cir. 1996), *vacated and remanded,* 521 U.S. 1114 (1997) (mem.), *on remand* 125 F.3d 1017 (7th Cir. 1997).

269. 85 F.3d 1050 (2nd Cir. 1996), *vacated and remanded,* 521 U.S. 1114 (1997) (mem.), *reversed and remanded on remand sub nom. Russman v. Mills,* 150 F.3d 219 (2nd Cir. 1998).

270. 107 F.3d 797 (10th Cir. 1997a), *vacated and remanded,* 521 U.S. 1115 (1997) (mem.), *on remand,* 129 F.3d 1431 (10th Cir. 1997).

271. *See Roslyn Union Free Sch. Dist. v. University of the State of N.Y., State Educ. Dep't,* 711 N.Y.S.2d 582 (N.Y. App. Div. 2000) (affirming that a school board was not required to provide a child with transportation to a private after school program on the basis that it had not denied the student access to its after school program).

272. 34 C.F.R. § 300.456(b).

273. 810 F. Supp. 1062 (E.D. Mo. 1993).

274. 117 F.3d 1371 (11th Cir. 1997).

275. 521 U.S. 1114 (1997) (mem.), *on remand* 125 F.3d 1017 (7th Cir. 1997).

276. *vacated and remanded,* 521 U.S. 1114 (1997) (mem.), *reversed and remanded on remand sub nom. Russman v. Mills,* 150 F.3d 219 (2nd Cir. 1998).

277. *vacated and remanded,* 521 U.S. 1115 (1997) (mem.), *on remand,* 129 F.3d 1431 (10th Cir. 1997).

278. 81 F.3d 673 (7th Cir. 1996), *vacated and remanded,* 521 U.S. 1114 (1997) (mem.).

279. 125 F.3d 1017 (7th Cir. 1997).

280. *Nieuwenhuis v. Delavan-Darien Sch. Dist. Bd. of Educ.,* 996 F. Supp. 855 (E.D. Wis. 1998).

281. 107 F.3d 797 (10th Cir. 1997).

282. 129 F.3d 1431 (10th Cir. 1997).

283. 85 F.3d 1050 (2nd Cir. 1996), *vacated and remanded,* 521 U.S. 1114 (1997) (mem.).

284. 150 F.3d 219 (2nd Cir. 1998). The name of the defendant changed when New York State named a new Commissioner of Education.

285. *Russman v. Board of Educ. of the Enlarged City Sch. Dist. of the City of Watervliet,* 92 F. Supp.2d 93 (N.D.N.Y. 2000).

286. 103 F.3d 393 (5th Cir. 1997) *withdrawn.*

287. 117 F.3d 231 (5th Cir. 1997), previous decision at 103 F.3d 393 (5th Cir. 1997) *withdrawn.*

288. 927 F. Supp. 1214 (E.D. Mo. 1996); *motion for reconsideration denied* 968 F. Supp. 481 (E.D. Mo. 1997), *aff'd* 153 F.3d 863 (8th Cir. 1998).

289. 155 F.3d 992 (8th Cir. 1998), *on remand Westendorp v. Independent Sch. Dist. No. 273,* 35 F. Supp.2d (Minn. 1998).

290. 35 F. Supp.2d 1134 (D. Minn. 1998).

291. 206 F.3d 813 (8th Cir. 2000).

292. 20 U.S.C. § 1412(a)(10)(A)(i)(I), 34 C.F.R.§ 300.453(a).

293. 34 C.F.R.§ 300.454.

294. 34 C.F.R. § 300.451.
295. *But see Board of Educ. of Kiryas Joel Village Sch. Dist. v. Grument,* 512 U.S. 687 (1994) (striking down the creation of a public school district to serve the needs of children with disabilities where its boundaries were identical to those of their religious community).
296. 34 C.F.R. § 300.456.
297. 34 C.F.R. § 300.451(b).
298. 34 C.F.R. § 300.457(a).
299. 34 C.F.R. § 300.456(b).
300. 34 C.F.R. § 300.453.
301. 34 C.F.R. § 300.455(a)(3).
302. *Id.*
303. 34 C.F.R. § 300.455(a)(1).
304. 34 C.F.R. § 300.455(a)(2).
305. 473 U.S. 402 (1985).
306. 521 U.S. 203 (1997).
307. *See* Charles J. Russo, & Allan G. Osborne, Jr., "*Agostini v. Felton*: Is the Demise of the Ghoul at Hand," *Education Law Reporter, Vol. 116, No. 2,* p. 515 (1997); Allan G. Osborne, Jr., & Charles J. Russo, "The Ghoul is Dead, Long Live the Ghoul: *Agostini v. Felton* and the Delivery of Title I Services in Nonpublic Schools," *Education Law Reporter, Vol. 119, No. 3,* p. 781 (1997).
308. United States Department of Education (1997, July). Guidance on the Supreme Court's Decision in *Agostini v. Felton* and Title I (Part A) of the Elementary and Secondary Education Act. http://www.ed.gov/legislation/ESEA/feltguid.html
309. For an interesting case relating to parental expectations, *see Ullmo v. Gilmour Academy,* 275 F.3d 671 (6th Cir. 2001) (affirming that the "philosophy" section in a Catholic school's parent handbook was insufficiently specific to create an enforceable promise under Ohio law after parents of a special education student were not satisfied with the education that he received).
310. *Tinker v. Des Moines Indep. Community Sch. Dist.,* 393 U.S. 503, 505 (1969) (upholding the free speech rights of students) ("[i]t can hardly be argued that either students or teachers shed their constitutional rights to freedom of speech or expression at the schoolhouse gate.")
311. Gerald M. Cattaro, "Collaboration and Constructivism; A Case Study for the Nonpublic Schools," *Curriculum Leadership: Rethinking Schools for the 21st Century,* Regis Bernhardt, Carolyn N. Headly, Gerald M. Cattaro, & Vasilios Svolopoulos, eds., (Cresskill, NJ: Hampton Press, 1997), pp. 69-88.
312. Luke 20:25.

Appendices

APPENDIX 1

Welcome and Justice
for Persons with Disabilities

A Framework of Access and Inclusion
A Statement of the U.S. Bishops

Twenty years ago we issued a statement calling for inclusion of persons with disabilities in the life of the Church and community. In 1982 the National Catholic Office for Persons with Disabilities was established to promote this ministry. And in 1995 we strengthened our commitment with passage of the *Guidelines for the Celebration of the Sacraments with Persons with Disabilities*.

This moral framework is based upon Catholic documents and serves as a guide for contemplation and action. We hope that the reaffirmation of the following principles will assist the faithful in bringing the principles of justice and inclusion to the many new and evolving challenges confronted by persons with disabilities today.

1. We are a single flock under the care of a single shepherd. There can be no separate Church for persons with disabilities.

2. Each person is created in God's image, yet there are variations in individual abilities. Positive recognition of these differences discourages discrimination and enhances the unity of the Body of Christ.

3. Our defense of life and rejection of the culture of death requires that we acknowledge the dignity and positive contributions of our brothers and sisters with disabilities. We unequivocally oppose negative attitudes toward disability which often lead to abortion, medical rationing, and euthanasia.

4. Defense of the right to life implies the defense of all other rights that enable individuals with disabilities to achieve the fullest measure of personal development of which they are capable. These include the right to equal opportunity in education, in employment, in housing, and in health care, as well as the rights to free access to public accommodations, facilities, and services.

5. Parish liturgical celebrations and catechetical programs should be accessible to persons with disabilities and open to their full, active, and conscious participation according to their capacity.

6. Since the parish is the door to participation in the Christian experience, it is the responsibility of both pastors and laity to assure that those doors are always open. Costs must never be the controlling consideration limiting the welcome offered to those among us with disabilities, since provision of access to religious functions is a pastoral duty.

7. We must recognize and appreciate the contributions that persons with disabilities can make to the Church's spiritual life and encourage them to do the Lord's work in the world according to their God-given talents and capacity.

8. We welcome qualified persons with disabilities to ordination, to consecrated life, and to full-time, professional service in the Church.

9. Often families are unprepared for the birth of a child with a disability or the development of impairments. Our pastoral response is to become informed about disabilities and to offer ongoing support to the family and welcome to the child.

10. Evangelization efforts are most effective when promoted by diocesan staff and parish committees that include persons with disabilities. Where no such evangelization efforts exist, we urge that they be developed.

We join the Holy Father in calling for actions that "ensure that the power of salvation may be shared by all" (John Paul II, *Tertio Millennio Adveniente*, n. 16). Furthermore, we encourage all Catholics to study the original U.S. bishops and Vatican documents from which these principles were drawn.

APPENDIX 2

Selected regulations,
34 C.F.R. §§ 300.400-300.462

Code of Federal Regulations
TITLE 34—EDUCATION

SUBPART D—CHILDREN IN PRIVATE SCHOOLS

CHILDREN WITH DISABILITIES IN PRIVATE SCHOOLS PLACED OR REFERRED
BY PUBLIC AGENCIES

Sec. 300.400 Applicability of Secs. 300.400-300.402.
Sections 300.401-300.402 apply only to children with disabilities who are or have been placed in or referred to a private school or facility by a public agency as a means of providing special education and related services.

(Authority: 20 U.S.C. 1412(a)(10)(B))

Sec. 300.401 Responsibility of State educational agency.
Each SEA shall ensure that a child with a disability who is placed in or referred to a private school or facility by a public agency—
(a) Is provided special education and related services—
(1) In conformance with an IEP that meets the requirements of Secs. 300.340-300.350; and
(2) At no cost to the parents;
(b) Is provided an education that meets the standards that apply to education provided by the SEA and LEAs (including the requirements of this part); and
(c) Has all of the rights of a child with a disability who is served by a public agency.

(Authority: 20 U.S.C. 1412(a)(10)(B))

Sec. 300.402 Implementation by State educational agency.

In implementing Sec. 300.401, the SEA shall—

(a) Monitor compliance through procedures such as written reports, on-site visits, and parent questionnaires;

(b) Disseminate copies of applicable standards to each private school and facility to which a public agency has referred or placed a child with a disability; and

(c) Provide an opportunity for those private schools and facilities to participate in the development and revision of State standards that apply to them.

(Authority: 20 U.S.C. 1412(a)(10)(B))

CHILDREN WITH DISABILITIES ENROLLED BY THEIR PARENTS IN PRIVATE SCHOOLS WHEN FAPE IS AT ISSUE

Sec. 300.403 Placement of children by parents if FAPE is at issue.

(a) General. This part does not require an LEA to pay for the cost of education, including special education and related services, of a child with a disability at a private school or facility if that agency made FAPE available to the child and the parents elected to place the child in a private school or facility. However, the public agency shall include that child in the population whose needs are addressed consistent with Secs. 300.450-300.462.

(b) Disagreements about FAPE. Disagreements between a parent and a public agency regarding the availability of a program appropriate for the child, and the question of financial responsibility, are subject to the due process procedures of Secs. 300.500-300.517.

(c) Reimbursement for private school placement. If the parents of a child with a disability, who previously received special education and related services under the authority of a public agency, enroll the child in a private preschool, elementary, or secondary school without the consent of or referral by the public agency, a court or a hearing officer may require the agency to reimburse the parents for the cost of that enrollment if the court or hearing officer finds that the agency had not made FAPE available to the child in a timely manner prior to that enrollment and that the private placement is appropriate. A parental placement may be found to be appropriate by a hearing officer or a court even if it does not meet the State standards that apply to education provided by the SEA and LEAs.

(d) Limitation on reimbursement. The cost of reimbursement described in paragraph (c) of this section may be reduced or denied—

(1) If—

(i) At the most recent IEP meeting that the parents attended prior to removal of the child from the public school, the parents did not inform the IEP team that they were rejecting the placement proposed by the public agency to provide FAPE to their child, including stating their concerns and their intent to enroll their child in a private school at public expense; or

(ii) At least ten (10) business days (including any holidays that occur on a business day) prior to the removal of the child from the public school, the parents did not give written notice to the public agency of the information described in paragraph (d)(1)(i) of this section;

(2) If, prior to the parents' removal of the child from the public school, the public agency informed the parents, through the notice requirements described in Sec. 300.503(a)(1), of its intent to evaluate the child (including a statement of the purpose of the evaluation that was appropriate and reasonable), but the parents did not make the child available for the evaluation; or

(3) Upon a judicial finding of unreasonableness with respect to actions taken by the parents.

(e) Exception. Notwithstanding the notice requirement in paragraph (d)(1) of this section, the cost of reimbursement may not be reduced or denied for failure to provide the notice if—

(1) The parent is illiterate and cannot write in English;

(2) Compliance with paragraph (d)(1) of this section would likely result in physical or serious emotional harm to the child;

(3) The school prevented the parent from providing the notice; or

(4) The parents had not received notice, pursuant to section 615 of the Act, of the notice requirement in paragraph (d)(1) of this section.

(Authority: 20 U.S.C. 1412(a)(10)(C))

CHILDREN WITH DISABILITIES ENROLLED BY THEIR PARENTS IN PRIVATE SCHOOLS

Sec. 300.450 Definition of "private school children with disabilities."

As used in this part, private school children with disabilities means children with disabilities enrolled by their parents in private schools or facilities other than children with disabilities covered under Secs. 300.400-300.402.

(Authority: 20 U.S.C. 1412(a)(10)(A))

Sec. 300.451 Child find for private school children with disabilities.

(a) Each LEA shall locate, identify, and evaluate all private school children with disabilities, including religious-school children residing in the jurisdiction of the LEA, in accordance with Secs. 300.125 and 300.220. The activities undertaken to carry out this responsibility for private school children with disabilities must be comparable to activities undertaken for children with disabilities in public schools.

(b) Each LEA shall consult with appropriate representatives of private school children with disabilities on how to carry out the activities described in paragraph (a) of this section.

(Authority: 20 U.S.C. 1412(a)(10)(A)(ii))

Sec. 300.452 Provision of services—basic requirement.

(a) General. To the extent consistent with their number and location in the State, provision must be made for the participation of private school children with disabilities in the program assisted or carried out under Part B of the Act by providing them with special education and related services in accordance with Secs. 300.453-300.462.

(b) SEA Responsibility—services plan. Each SEA shall ensure that, in accordance with paragraph (a) of this section and Secs. 300.454-300.456, a services plan is developed and implemented for each private school child with a disability who has been designated to receive special education and related services under this part.

(Authority: 20 U.S.C. 1412(a)(10)(A)(i))

Sec. 300.453 Expenditures.

(a) Formula. To meet the requirement of Sec. 300.452(a), each LEA must spend on providing special education and related services to private school children with disabilities—

(1) For children aged 3 through 21, an amount that is the same proportion of the LEA's total subgrant under section 611(g) of the Act as the number of private school children with disabilities aged 3 through 21 residing in its jurisdiction is to the total number of children with disabilities in its jurisdiction aged 3 through 21; and

(2) For children aged 3 through 5, an amount that is the same proportion of the LEA's total subgrant under section 619(g) of the Act as the number of private school children with disabilities aged 3 through 5 residing in its jurisdiction is to the total number of children with disabilities in its jurisdiction aged 3 through 5.

(b) Child count.

(1) Each LEA shall—

(i) Consult with representatives of private school children in deciding how to conduct the annual count of the number of private school children with disabilities; and

(ii) Ensure that the count is conducted on December 1 or the last Friday of October of each year.

(2) The child count must be used to determine the amount that the LEA must spend on providing special education and related services to private school children with disabilities in the next subsequent fiscal year.

(c) Expenditures for child find may not be considered. Expenditures for child find activities described in Sec. 300.451 may not be considered in determining whether the LEA has met the requirements of paragraph (a) of this section.

(d) Additional services permissible. State and local educational agencies are not prohibited from providing services to private school children with disabilities in excess of those required by this part, consistent with State law or local policy.

(Authority: 20 U.S.C. 1412(a)(10)(A))

Sec. 300.454 Services determined.

(a) No individual right to special education and related services.

(1) No private school child with a disability has an individual right to receive some or all of the special education and related services that the child would receive if enrolled in a public school.

(2) Decisions about the services that will be provided to private school children with disabilities under Secs. 300.452-300.462, must be made in accordance with paragraphs (b), and (c) of this section.

(b) Consultation with representatives of private school children with disabilities. (1) General. Each LEA shall consult, in a timely and meaningful way, with appropriate representatives of private school children with disabilities in light of the funding under Sec. 300.453, the number of private school children with disabilities, the needs of private school children with disabilities, and their location to decide—

(i) Which children will receive services under Sec. 300.452;

(ii) What services will be provided;

(iii) How and where the services will be provided; and

(iv) How the services provided will be evaluated.

(2) Genuine opportunity. Each LEA shall give appropriate representatives of private school children with disabilities a genuine opportunity to express their views regarding each matter that is subject to the consultation requirements in this section.

(3) Timing. The consultation required by paragraph (b)(1) of this section must occur before the LEA makes any decision that affects the opportunities of private school children with disabilities to participate in services under Secs. 300.452-300.462.

(4) Decisions. The LEA shall make the final decisions with respect to the services to be provided to eligible private school children.

(c) Services plan for each child served under Secs. 300.450-300.462. If a child with a disability is enrolled in a religious or other private school and will receive special education or related services from an LEA, the LEA shall—

(1) Initiate and conduct meetings to develop, review, and revise a services plan for the child, in accordance with Sec. 300.455(b); and

(2) Ensure that a representative of the religious or other private school attends each meeting. If the representative cannot attend, the

LEA shall use other methods to ensure participation by the private school, including individual or conference telephone calls.

(Authority: 1412(a)(10)(A))

Sec. 300.455 Services provided.

(a) General.

(1) The services provided to private school children with disabilities must be provided by personnel meeting the same standards as personnel providing services in the public schools.

(2) Private school children with disabilities may receive a different amount of services than children with disabilities in public schools.

(3) No private school child with a disability is entitled to any service or to any amount of a service the child would receive if enrolled in a public school.

(b) Services provided in accordance with a services plan. (1) Each private school child with a disability who has been designated to receive services under Sec. 300.452 must have a services plan that describes the specific special education and related services that the LEA will provide to the child in light of the services that the LEA has determined, through the process described in Secs. 300.453-300.454, it will make available to private school children with disabilities.

(2) The services plan must, to the extent appropriate—

(i) Meet the requirements of Sec. 300.347, with respect to the services provided; and

(ii) Be developed, reviewed, and revised consistent with Secs. 300.342-300.346.

(Authority: 20 U.S.C. 1412(a)(10)(A))

Sec. 300.456 Location of services; transportation.

(a) On-site. Services provided to private school children with disabilities may be provided on-site at a child's private school, including a religious school, to the extent consistent with law.

(b) Transportation.

(1) General.

(i) If necessary for the child to benefit from or participate in the services provided under this part, a private school child with a disability must be provided transportation—

(A) From the child's school or the child's home to a site other than the private school; and

(B) From the service site to the private school, or to the child's home, depending on the timing of the services.

(ii) LEAs are not required to provide transportation from the child's home to the private school.

(2) Cost of transportation. The cost of the transportation described in paragraph (b)(1)(i) of this section may be included in calculating whether the LEA has met the requirement of Sec. 300.453.

(Authority: 20 U.S.C. 1412(a)(10)(A))

Sec. 300.457 Complaints.

(a) Due process inapplicable. The procedures in Secs. 300.504-300.515 do not apply to complaints that an LEA has failed to meet the requirements of Secs. 300.452-300.462, including the provision of services indicated on the child's services plan.

(b) Due process applicable. The procedures in Secs. 300.504-300.515 do apply to complaints that an LEA has failed to meet the requirements of Sec. 300.451, including the requirements of Secs. 300.530-300.543.

(c) State complaints. Complaints that an SEA or LEA has failed to meet the requirements of Secs. 300.451-300.462 may be filed under the procedures in Secs. 300.660-300.662.

(Authority: 20 U.S.C. 1412(a)(10)(A))

Sec. 300.458 Separate classes prohibited.

An LEA may not use funds available under section 611 or 619 of the Act for classes that are organized separately on the basis of school enrollment or religion of the students if—

(a) The classes are at the same site; and

(b) The classes include students enrolled in public schools and students enrolled in private schools.

(Authority: 20 U.S.C. 1412(a)(10)(A))

Sec. 300.459 Requirement that funds not benefit a private school.

(a) An LEA may not use funds provided under section 611 or 619 of the Act to finance the existing level of instruction in a private school or to otherwise benefit the private school.

(b) The LEA shall use funds provided under Part B of the Act to meet the special education and related services needs of students enrolled in private schools, but not for—

(1) The needs of a private school; or

(2) The general needs of the students enrolled in the private school.

(Authority: 20 U.S.C. 1412(a)(10)(A))

Sec. 300.460 Use of public school personnel.

An LEA may use funds available under sections 611 and 619 of the Act to make public school personnel available in other than public facilities—

(a) To the extent necessary to provide services under Secs. 300.450-300.462 for private school children with disabilities; and

(b) If those services are not normally provided by the private school.

(Authority: 20 U.S.C. 1412(a)(10)(A))

Sec. 300.461 Use of private school personnel.

An LEA may use funds available under section 611 or 619 of the Act to pay for the services of an employee of a private school to provide services under Secs. 300.450-300.462 if—

(a) The employee performs the services outside of his or her regular hours of duty; and

(b) The employee performs the services under public supervision and control.

(Authority: 20 U.S.C. 1412(a)(10)(A))

Sec. 300.462 Requirements concerning property, equipment, and supplies for the benefit of private school children with disabilities.

(a) A public agency must keep title to and exercise continuing administrative control of all property, equipment, and supplies that the public agency acquires with funds under section 611 or 619 of the Act for the benefit of private school children with disabilities.

(b) The public agency may place equipment and supplies in a private school for the period of time needed for the program.

(c) The public agency shall ensure that the equipment and supplies placed in a private school—

(1) Are used only for Part B purposes; and

(2) Can be removed from the private school without remodeling the private school facility.

(d) The public agency shall remove equipment and supplies from a private school if—

(1) The equipment and supplies are no longer needed for Part B purposes; or

(2) Removal is necessary to avoid unauthorized use of the equipment and supplies for other than Part B purposes.

(e) No funds under Part B of the Act may be used for repairs, minor remodeling, or construction of private school facilities.

(Authority: 20 U.S.C. 1412(a)(10)(A))

APPENDIX 3

Useful Special Education Web Sites

http://www.ed.gov/offices/OSERS/IDEA/
This site of the United States Department of Education contains updates on regulations, articles, and other general information on the IDEA.

http://www.ed.gov/offices/OIIA/NonPublic/faqs.html
This site contains questions and answers on special education services under the IDEA for non-public schools.

http://seriweb.com
This site includes internet accessible information on special education.

http://www.specialednews.com
This site includes current news articles on special education.

http://www.iser.com
This site provides links to many other useful sites.

http://web.nysed.gov/vesid/sped/spedmain.html
This site provides useful information on special education in New York.

http://www.state.nj.us/njded/specialed/
This site provides useful information on special education in New Jersey.

http://www.ideapractices.org/
This site provides articles, information, ideas, and links to other sites.

http://www.dssc.org/frc/idea.htm
This site is easy to navigate and contains much useful information.

http://www.protectionandadvocacy.com/idea2.htm
This site includes questions and answers which make it easier to understand IDEA and how it differs from other laws regarding special education.

http://curry.edschool.virginia.edu/go/cise/ose/resources/legal.html
This site provides links on special education and students with disabilities.

http://www.specialedlaw.net/index.mv
This site provides information on the law of special education.

http://www.irsc.org/laws.htm
This site provides internet resources for children as well as links and articles on the law of special education.

http://www.wrightslaw.com/
This site includes articles, cases, newsletters, and other information about special education law.

http://www.napsec.com/
This site includes material from the National Association of Private Special Education Centers, a non-profit association whose mission is to represent private special education programs and affiliated state associations.

About the Authors

Charles J. Russo, MDiv, JD, EdD, is the Panzer Chair in Education in the School of Education and Allied Professions and an Adjunct Professor in the School of Law at the University of Dayton.

Rev. Joseph D. Massucci. PhD, is Chair of the Department of Educational Leadership in the School of Education and Allied Professions at the University of Dayton.

Allan G. Osborne, Jr., EdD, is Principal at Snug Harbor Community School and Visiting Associate Professor at Bridgewater State College.

Gerald M. Cattaro, EdD, is an Associate Professor in the Division of Administration, Policy, and Urban Education and Director of the Center for Non-Public Education and Catholic School Leadership at Fordham University.